Widmaier

3 - 50

125 - 202

republic.com

republic.com

cass sunstein

princeton university press
princeton and oxford

Library of Congress Cataloging-in-Publication Data

Sunstein, Cass R.
Republic.com / Cass R. Sunstein.
p.   cm.
Includes bibliographical references and index.
ISBN 0-691-07025-3 (alk. paper)
1. Information society.   2.Information society—
Political aspects.   3. Internet—Social aspects
4. Control (Psychology)   I. Title.
HM851 .S87 2001
303.48'33—dc21   00-045331

This book has been composed in Monotype Centaur
Designed by Grady Klein
Composed by Gretchen Oberfranc

The paper used in this publication meets the minimum
requirements of ANSI/NISO Z39.48-1992
(R1997) (*Permanence of Paper*)

www.pup.princeton.edu

Printed in the United States of America

10   9   8   7   6   5   4   3   2   1

for mn

The "TV guide" will almost be like a search portal where you'll customize and say, "I'm never interested in this, but I am particularly interested in that." It's already getting a little unwieldy. When you turn on DirectTV and you step through every channel—well, there's three minutes of your life. When you walk into your living room six years from now, you'll be able to just say what you're interested in, and have the screen help you pick out a video that you care about. It's not going to be "Let's look at channels 4, 5, and 7." It's going to be something that has pretty incredible graphics and it's got an Internet connection to it.

- Bill Gates

What is more significant is that counting of heads compels prior recourse to methods of discussion, consultation and persuasion, while the essence of appeal to force is to cut short resort to such methods. Majority rule, just as majority rule, is as foolish as its critics charge it with being. But it never is *merely* majority rule. . . . The important consideration is that opportunity be given ideas to speak and to become the possession of the multitude. The essential need is the improvement of the methods and constitution of debate, discussion and persuasion. That is *the* problem of the public.

- John Dewey, *The Public and its Problems*

Television is just another appliance. It's a toaster with pictures.

- Mark Fowler, former Chair of the Federal Communications Commission

One must take men as they are, they tell us, and not as the world's uninformed pedants or good-natured dreamers fancy that they ought to be. But "as they are" ought to read "as we have made them." . . . In this way, the prophecy of the supposedly clever statesmen is fulfilled.

●   Immanuel Kant, *The Contest of Faculties*

contents

CHAPTER 1 ● The Daily Me   3

CHAPTER 2 ● An Analogy and an Ideal   23

CHAPTER 3 ● Fragmentation and Cybercascades   51

CHAPTER 4 ● Social Glue and Spreading Information   89

CHAPTER 5 ● Citizens   105

CHAPTER 6 ● What's Regulation? A Plea   125

CHAPTER 7 ● Freedom of Speech   141

CHAPTER 8 ● Policies and Proposals   167

CHAPTER 9 ● Conclusion: Republic.com   191

         Bibliographical Note   203

         Notes   205

         Acknowledgments   213

         Index   215

republic.com

the daily me

It is some time in the future. Technology has greatly increased people's ability to "filter" what they want to read, see, and hear. General interest newspapers and magazines are largely a thing of the past. The same is true of broadcasters. The idea of choosing "channel 4" or instead "channel 7" seems positively quaint. With the aid of a television or computer screen, and the Internet, you are able to design your own newspapers and magazines. Having dispensed with broadcasters, you can choose your own video programming, with movies, game shows, sports, shopping, and news of your choice. You mix and match.

You need not come across topics and views that you have not sought out. Without any difficulty, you are able to see exactly what you want to see, no more and no less.

Maybe you want to focus on sports all the time, and to avoid anything dealing with business or government. It is easy for you to do exactly that. Perhaps you choose replays of famous football games in the early evening, live baseball from New York at night, and college basketball on the weekends. If you hate sports, and want to learn about the Middle East in the evening and watch old situation comedies late at night, that is easy too. If you care only

3

about the United States, and want to avoid international issues entirely, you can restrict yourself to material involving the United States. So too if you care only about New York, or Chicago, or California, or Long Island.

Perhaps you have no interest at all in "news." Maybe you find "news" impossibly boring. If so, you need not see it at all. Maybe you select programs and stories involving only music and weather. Or perhaps you are more specialized still, emphasizing opera, or Beethoven, or the Rolling Stones, or modern dance, or some subset of one or more of the above.

If you are interested in politics, you may want to restrict yourself to certain points of view, by hearing only from people you like. In designing your preferred newspaper, you choose among conservatives, moderates, liberals, vegetarians, the religious right, and socialists. You have your favorite columnists; perhaps you want to hear from them, and from no one else. If so, that is entirely feasible with a simple "point and click." Or perhaps you are interested in only a few topics. If you believe that the most serious problem is gun control, or global warming, or lung cancer, you might spend most of your time reading about that problem, if you wish from the point of view that you like best.

Of course everyone else has the same freedom that you do. Many people choose to avoid news altogether. Many people restrict themselves to their own preferred points of view—liberals watching and reading mostly or only liberals; moderates, moderates; conservatives, conservatives; neo-Nazis, neo-Nazis. People in different states, and in different countries, make predictably different choices.

The resulting divisions run along many lines—of race, religion, ethnicity, nationality, wealth, age, political conviction, and more. Most whites avoid news and entertainment options designed for African-Americans. Many African-Americans focus largely on options specifically designed for them. So too with Hispanics. With the reduced importance of the general interest *magazine and newspaper, and the flowering of individual programming design, different groups make fundamentally different choices.*

The market for news, entertainment, and information has finally been perfected. Consumers are able to see exactly what they want. When the power to filter is unlimited, people can decide, in advance and with perfect accuracy, what they will and will not encounter. They can design something very much like a communications universe of their own choosing.

PERSONALIZATION AND DEMOCRACY

Our communications market is rapidly moving in the direction of this apparently utopian picture. As of this writing, many newspapers, including the *Wall Street Journal*, allow readers to create "personalized" electronic editions, containing exactly what they want, and excluding what they do not want. If you are interested in getting help with the design of an entirely personalized paper, you can consult an ever-growing number of Websites, including individual.com (helpfully named!) and crayon.com (a less helpful name, but evocative in its own way).

In reality, we are not so very far from complete personalization of the system of communications. Consider just a few examples.

> • Broadcast.com has "compiled hundreds of thousands of programs so you can find the one that suits your fancy. . . . For example, if you want to see all the latest fashions from France twenty-four hours of the day you can get them. If you're from Baltimore living in Dallas

and you want to listen to WBAL, your hometown station, you can hear it."[1]

● Sonicnet.com allows you to create your own musical universe, consisting of what it calls "Me Music." Me Music is a "place where you can listen to the music you love on the radio station YOU create . . . A place where you can watch videos of your favorite artists and new artists."

● Zatso.com allows users to produce "a personal newscast." Its intention is to create a place "where you decide what's news." Your task is to tell "what TV news stories you're interested in," and Zatso.com turns that information into a specifically designed newscast. From the main "This is the News I Want" menu, you can choose stories with particular words and phrases, or you can select topics, such as sports, weather, crime, health, government/politics, and much more.

● Info Xtra offers "news and entertainment that's important to you," and it allows you to find this "without hunting through newspapers, radio and websites." Personalized news, local weather, and "even your daily horoscope or winning lottery number" will be delivered to you once you specify what you want and when you want it.

● TiVo, a television recording system, is designed, in the words of its Website, to give "you the ultimate control over your TV viewing." It does this by putting "you at the center of your own TV network, so you'll always have access to whatever you want, whenever you want." TiVo "will automatically find and digitally record your favorite programs every time they air" and will help you create "your personal TV line-up." It will also learn your tastes, so that it can "suggest other shows that you may want to record and watch based on your preferences."

● Intertainer, Inc. provides "home entertainment services on demand," not limited to television but also including music, movies, and shopping. Intertainer is intended for people who want "total control" and "personalized experiences." It is "a new way to get whatever movies, music, and television you want anytime you want on your PC or TV."

● George Bell, the chief executive officer of the search engine Excite, exclaims, "We are looking for ways to be able to lift chunks of content off other areas of our service and paste them onto your personal page so you can constantly refresh and update that 'newspaper of me.' About 43 percent of our entire user data base has personalized their experience on Excite."[2]

If you put the words "personalized news" in any search engine, you will find vivid evidence of what is happening. And that is only the tip of the iceberg.[3] Thus MIT technology specialist Nicholas Negroponte prophecies the emergence of "the Daily Me"—a communications package that is personally designed, with each component fully chosen in advance.[4] Many of us are applauding these developments, which obviously increase individual convenience and entertainment. But in the midst of the applause, we should insist on asking some questions. How will the increasing power of private

7

control affect democracy? How will the Internet, the new forms of television, and the explosion of communications options alter the capacity of citizens to govern themselves? What are the social preconditions for a well-functioning system of democratic deliberation, or for individual freedom itself?

My purpose in this book is to cast some light on these questions. I do so by emphasizing the most striking power provided by emerging technologies: *the growing power of consumers to filter what they see.* In the process of discussing this power, I will attempt to provide a better understanding of the meaning of freedom of speech in a democratic society. I will also outline possible policy reforms, designed to ensure that new communications technologies serve democracy, rather than the other way around.

A large part of my aim is to explore what makes for a well-functioning system of free expression. Above all, I urge that in a diverse society, such a system requires far more than restraints on government censorship and respect for individual choices. For the last decades, this has been the preoccupation of American law and politics, and indeed the law and politics of many other nations as well, including, for example, Germany, France, England, and Israel. Censorship is indeed a threat to democracy and freedom. But an exclusive focus on government censorship produces serious blind spots. In particular, a well-functioning system of free expression must meet two distinctive requirements.

First, people should be exposed to materials that they would not have chosen in advance. Unplanned, unanticipated encounters are central to democracy itself. Such encounters often involve topics and points of view that people have not

8 *who chooses it?*

sought out and perhaps find quite irritating. They are important partly to ensure against fragmentation and extremism, which are predictable outcomes of any situation in which like-minded people speak only with themselves. I do not suggest that government should force people to see things that they wish to avoid. But I do contend that in a democracy deserving the name, people often come across views and topics that they have not specifically selected.

Second, many or most citizens should have a range of common experiences. Without shared experiences, a heterogeneous society will have a much more difficult time in addressing social problems. People may even find it hard to understand one another. Common experiences, emphatically including the common experiences made possible by the media, provide a form of social glue. A system of communications that radically diminishes the number of such experiences will create a number of problems, not least because of the increase in social fragmentation.

As preconditions for a well-functioning democracy, these requirements hold in any large nation. They are especially important in a heterogeneous nation, one that faces an occasional risk of fragmentation. They have all the more importance as each nation becomes increasingly global and each citizen becomes, to a greater or lesser degree, a "citizen of the world."[5]

An insistence on these two requirements should not be rooted in nostalgia for some supposedly idyllic past. With respect to communications, the past was hardly idyllic. Compared to any other period in human history, we are in the midst of many extraordinary gains, not least from the standpoint of democracy itself. For us, nostalgia is not only unproductive but also senseless. Nor should anything here be taken as a reason for "optimism" or "pessimism," two great obstacles to clear thinking about new technological developments. If we must choose between them, by all means let us choose optimism. But in view of the many potential gains and losses inevitably associated with massive technological change, any attitude of "optimism" or "pessimism" is far too general to make sense. What I mean to provide is not a basis for pessimism, but a lens through which we might understand, a bit better than before, what makes a system of freedom of expression successful in the first place. That improved understanding will equip us to appreciate a free nation's own aspirations and thus help in evaluating continuing changes in the system of communications. It will also point the way toward a clearer understanding of the nature of citizenship and toward social reforms if emerging developments disserve our aspirations, as they threaten to do.

central thesis

As we shall see, it is much too simple to say that any system of communications is desirable if and because it allows individuals to see and hear what they choose. Unanticipated, unchosen exposures, and shared experiences, are important too.

PRECURSORS AND INTERMEDIARIES

Unlimited filtering may seem quite strange, perhaps even the stuff of science fiction. But it is not entirely different from what has come before. Filtering is inevitable, a fact of life. It is as old as humanity itself. No one can see, hear, or read everything. In the course of any hour, let alone any day, every one of us engages in massive filtering, simply to make life manageable and coherent.

With respect to the world of communications, moreover, a free society gives people a great deal of power to filter out unwanted materials. Only tyrannies force people to read or to watch. In free nations, those who read newspapers do not read the same newspaper; some people do not read any newspaper at all. Every day, people make choices among magazines based on their tastes and their point of view. Sports enthusiasts choose sports magazines, and in many nations they can choose a magazine focused on the sport of their choice, *Basketball Weekly*, say, or the *Practical Horseman*; conservatives can read *National Review* or the *Weekly Standard*; countless magazines are available for those who like cars; *Dog Fancy* is a popular item for canine enthusiasts; people who are somewhat left of center might like the *American Prospect*; there is even a magazine called *Cigar Aficionado*.

These are simply contemporary illustrations of a long standing fact of life in democratic countries: a diversity of communications options and a range of possible choices. But the emerging situation does contain large differences, stemming above all from a dramatic increase in available options, a simultaneous increase in individual control over content, and a corresponding decrease in the power of *general interest intermediaries*.[6] These include newspapers, magazines, and broadcasters. An appreciation of the social functions of general interest intermediaries will play a large role in this book.

People who rely on such intermediaries have a range of chance encounters, involving shared experiences with diverse

empirical foundation of his argument
general intermediaries

others, and also exposure to materials and topics that they did not seek out in advance. You might, for example, read the city newspaper and in the process find a range of stories that you would not have selected if you had the power to do so. Your eyes might come across a story about ethnic tensions in Germany, or crime in Los Angeles, or innovative business practices in Tokyo, and you might read those stories although you would hardly have placed them in your "Daily Me." You might watch a particular television channel—perhaps you prefer channel 4—and when your favorite program ends, you might see the beginning of another show, perhaps a drama that you would not have chosen in advance but that somehow catches your eye. Reading *Time* or *Newsweek*, you might come across a discussion of endangered species in Madagascar, and this discussion might interest you, even affect your behavior, maybe even change your life, although you would not have sought it out in the first instance. A system in which individuals lack control over the particular content that they see has a great deal in common with a public street, where you might encounter not only friends, but also a heterogeneous array of people engaged in a wide array of activities (including perhaps bank presidents and political protesters and panhandlers).

Some people believe that the mass media are dying—that the whole idea of general interest intermediaries, providing both shared experiences for millions and exposure to diverse topics and ideas, was a short episode in the history of human communications. As a prediction, this view is probably overstated. But certainly the significance of the mass media has been decreasing over time. We should not forget that from the standpoint of human history, even in industrialized societies, general interest intermediaries are relatively new, and far from inevitable. Newspapers, radio stations, and television broadcasters have particular histories with distinctive beginnings and possibly distinctive endings. In fact the twentieth century should be seen as the great era for the general interest intermediary, providing similar information and entertainment to millions of people.

The twenty-first century may well be altogether different on this score. Consider one small fact: In 1948, daily newspaper circulation was 1.3 per household, a rate that had fallen by 57 percent by 1998—even though the number of years of education, typically correlated with newspaper readership, rose sharply in that period.[7] At the very least, the sheer volume of options, and the power to customize, are sharply diminishing the social role of the general interest intermediary.

POLITICS, FREEDOM, AND FILTERING

In the course of the discussion, we will encounter many issues. Each will be treated in some detail, but for the sake of convenience, here is a quick catalogue:

● the large difference between pure populism, or direct democracy, and a democratic system that attempts to ensure deliberation and reflection as well as accountability;

● the intimate relationship between free speech rights and social well-being, which such rights often serve;[8]

13

- the pervasive risk that discussion among like-minded people will breed excessive confidence, extremism, contempt for others, and sometimes even violence;
- the potentially dangerous role of social cascades, including "cybercascades," in which information, whether true or false, spreads like wildfire;
- the enormous potential of the Internet and other communications technologies in promoting freedom, in both poor and rich countries;
- the utterly implausible nature of the view that free speech is an "absolute";
- the ways in which information provided to any one of us is likely to benefit many of us;
- the critical difference between our role as citizens and our role as consumers;
- the inevitability of regulation of speech, indeed the inevitability of speech regulation benefiting those who most claim to be opposed to "regulation";
- the extent to which the extraordinary consumption opportunities created by the Internet do not really improve people's lives, because for many goods, they merely accelerate the "consumption treadmill"; and
- the potentially destructive effects of intense market pressures on both culture and government.

But the unifying issue throughout will be the various problems, for a democratic society, that might be created by the power of complete filtering. One question, which I answer in the affirmative, is whether individual choices, innocuous and perfectly reasonable in themselves, might produce a large set of social difficulties. Another question, which I also answer in the affirmative, is whether it is important to maintain the equivalent of "street corners," or "commons," where people are exposed to things quite involuntarily. More particularly, I seek to defend a particular conception of democracy—a deliberative conception—and to evaluate, in its terms, the outcome of a system with the power of perfect filtering. I also mean to defend a conception of freedom, associated with the deliberative conception of democracy, and to oppose it to a conception that sees consumption choices by individuals as the very embodiment of freedom.

My claim is emphatically not that street corners and general interest intermediaries will or would disappear in a world of perfect filtering. To what extent the market will produce them, or their equivalents, is an empirical issue. Many people like surprises. Some people have a strong taste for street corners and for their equivalent on the television and on the Internet. Indeed, new technological options hold out a great deal of promise for exposure to materials that used to be too hard to find, including new topics and new points of view. If you would like to find out about different forms of cancer, and different views about possible treatments, you can do so in less than a minute. If you are interested in learning about the risks associated with different automobiles, a quick search will tell you a great deal. If you would like to know about a particular foreign country, from its customs to its politics to its weather, you can do better with the Internet than you could have done with the best of encyclopedias.

Most parents of school-age children are stunned to see how easy all this is. From the standpoint of those concerned with ensuring access to more opinions and more topics, the new communications technologies can be a terrific boon. But it remains true that many apparent street corners, on the Internet in particular, are highly specialized. Consider Townhall.com, a street corner–type site, as befits its name, through which you can have access to dozens of sites. But unlike at most real townhalls, only conservative views can be found at Townhall.com. Each site is a conservative political organization of one sort or another, including, among many others, the American Conservative Union, the Oliver North Radio Show, Protect Americans Now, Conservative Political Action Conference, Citizens Against Government Waste, and the *National Review*—each with a site of its own, most with many links to like-minded sites, and few with links to opposing views.

What I will argue is not that people lack curiosity or that street corners will disappear but instead that there is an insistent need for them, and that a system of freedom of expression should be viewed partly in light of that need. What I will also suggest is that there are serious dangers in a system in which individuals bypass general interest intermediaries and restrict themselves to opinions and topics of their own choosing. In particular, I will emphasize the risks posed by any situation in which thousands or perhaps millions or even tens of millions of people are mainly listening to louder echoes of their own voices. A situation of this kind is likely to produce far worse than mere fragmentation.

[handwritten margin note: Risk definition here: consumers are the risk carriers]

WHAT IS AND WHAT ISN'T THE ISSUE

Some clarifications, designed to narrow the issue, are now in order. I will be stressing problems on the "demand" side on the speech market. These are problems that stem not from the actions of *producers*—Microsoft, Netscape, and the like—but instead from the choices and preferences of *consumers*. I am aware that on the standard view, the most important emerging problems come from large corporations, and not from the many millions, indeed billions, of individuals who make communications choices. In the long run, however, I believe that the more serious risks, and certainly the most neglected ones, are consumer driven. This is not because consumers are usually confused or irrational or malevolent. It is because choices that seem perfectly reasonable in isolation may, when taken together, badly disserve democratic goals.

Because of my focus on the consumers of information, I will not be discussing a wide range of issues that have engaged attention in the last decade. Many of these issues involve the allegedly excessive power of large corporations or conglomerates.

- I will not deal with the feared disappearance of coverage of issues of interest to small or disadvantaged groups. That is not likely to be a problem. On the contrary, there has been a tremendous growth in "niche markets," serving groups both large and small. With a decrease in scarcity, this trend will inevitably continue. Technological development is a great ally of small groups and minorities, however defined. People with unusual or specialized tastes are not likely to be frozen out of the emerging communications universe. The opposite is much more likely to be true; they will have easy access to their preferred fare, far easier than ever before. Hence that will be my focus here.

● I will provide little discussion of monopolistic behavior by suppliers or manipulative practices by them. That question has received considerable attention, above all in connection with the 1999–2000 antitrust litigation involving Microsoft. Undoubtedly some suppliers do try to monopolize, and some do try to manipulate; consider, for example, the fact that Netscape provides some automatic bookmarks, designed to allow users to link with certain sites but not others. (My own automatic bookmarks, for example, include ABC News and CBS Sportsline—not NBC or CBS news, and nothing from ABC or NBC sports.) All sensible producers of communications know that a degree of filtering is a fact of life. They also know something equally important but less obvious: Consumers' *attention* is the crucial (and scarce) commodity in the emerging market. Companies stand to gain a great deal if they can shift attention in one direction rather than another.

This is why many Internet sites provide information and entertainment to consumers for free. Consumers are actually a commodity, often "sold" to advertisers in return for money; it is therefore advertisers and not consumers who pay. This is pervasively true of radio and television.[9] To a large degree, it is true of websites too. Consider, for example, the hilarious case of Netzero. com, which provides free Internet access. Netzero.com describes itself—indeed this is its motto—as "Defender of the Free World." In an extensive advertising campaign, Netzero.com portrays its founders as besieged witnesses before a legislative committee, defending basic liberty by protecting everyone's "right" to have access to the Internet. But is Netzero.com really attempting to protect rights, or is it basically interested in earning profits? The truth is that Netzero.com is one of a number of for-profit companies, giving free Internet access to consumers (a social benefit to be sure), but making money by promising advertisers that the consumers it serves will see their commercials. There is nothing wrong with making money, but Netzero.com should hardly be seen as some dissident organization of altruistic patriots.

Especially in light of the overriding importance of attention, some private companies will attempt to manipulate consumers, and occasionally they will engage in monopolistic practices. Is this a problem? No unqualified answer would make sense. An important question is whether market forces will reduce the adverse effects of efforts at manipulation or monopoly. I believe that to a large extent, they will; but that is not my concern here. For a democracy, many of the most serious issues raised by the new technologies do not involve manipulation or monopolistic behavior by large companies.

• I will be discussing private power over "code," the structure and design of programs. In an illuminating and important book, Lawrence Lessig has expressed concern that private code-makers will control possibilities on the Internet, in a way that compromises privacy, the free circulation of ideas, and other important social values.[10] As Lessig persuasively demonstrates, this is indeed a possible problem. But the problem should not be overstated, particularly in view of the continuing effects of extraordinary competitive forces. The movement for "open code" (above all Linux), allowing people to design code as they wish, is flourishing, and in any case competitive pressures impose real limits on the extent to which code-makers may move in directions that consumers reject. Privacy guarantees, for example, are an emerging force on the Internet. Undoubtedly there is room, in some contexts, for a governmental role in ensuring against the abusive exercise of the private power over code. But that is not my concern in this book.

● I will not be discussing the "digital divide," at least not as this term is ordinarily understood. People concerned about this problem emphasize the existing inequality in access to new communications technologies, an inequality that divides, for example, those with and those without access to the Internet. That is indeed an important issue, not least domestically. According to recent estimates, income is the most significant source of the domestic divide; fewer than half of households with average incomes under $15,000 (19 percent of the total American population) will have entered the Internet population by as late as 2005. A large gap can also be found among ethnic groups, with African-American and Hispanic-American segments at 30 percent and 33 percent, respectively, in 1995, and whites well above 50 percent. But this gap is closing quickly, and it is anticipated that much of it will disappear by 2005.

The digital divide is far more serious internationally, because it threatens to aggravate existing social inequalities, many of them unjust, at the same time that it deprives many millions (in fact, billions) of people of information and opportunities. In 1998, for example, industrial countries, accounting for less than 15 percent of all people, had 88 percent of Internet users—with North America, home to less than 5 percent of the world's people, having more than half of its Internet users. In several African countries, the cost of a monthly Internet connection is as much as $100, ten times that in the United States. A computer would cost the average American about a month's wage, whereas it would cost a citizen of Bangladesh over eight years' income. In 2000, an astonishingly low 0.11 percent of the total Arab population had Internet access, at the same time when well over 50 percent of Americans, or 130 million people, had such access, with eighty million turning out to be active Internet users. But as in the domestic context, that problem seems likely to diminish over time. Of course we should do whatever we can to accelerate the process, which will provide benefits, not least for both freedom and health, for millions and even billions. But what I will describe will operate even if everyone is on the right side of that divide, that is, even if everyone has access to all media.

My focus, then, will be on several sorts of "digital divides" that are likely to emerge in the presence of universal access—on how reasonable choices by individual consumers might produce both individual and social harm. This point is emphatically connected with inequalities, but not in access to technologies; it does not depend in any way on inequalities there.

The digital divides that I will emphasize may or may not be a nightmare. But if I am right, there is all the reason in the world to reject the view that free markets, as embodied in the notion of "consumer sovereignty," are the appropriate foundation for communications policy. The imagined world of innumerable, diverse editions of the "Daily Me" is the furthest thing from a utopian dream, and it would create serious problems from the democratic point of view.

central

2

an analogy
and
an ideal

THE NEIGHBORHOOD ME

The changes now being produced by new communications technologies are understated, not overstated, by the thought experiment with which I began. What is happening goes far beyond the increasingly customized computer screen.

For countless people, the Internet is producing a substantial decrease in unanticipated, unchosen interactions with others. Many of us telecommute rather than going to work; this is a rapidly growing trend. Rather than visiting the local bookstore, where we are likely to see a number of diverse people, many of us shop for books on Amazon.com. Others avoid the video store or the grocery because Kosmo.com is entirely delighted to deliver *Citizen Kane* and a pizza. Because of MP3 technology, a visit to the local music store may well seem a hopeless waste of time. Thus communications specialist Ken Auletta enthuses, "I can sample music on my computer, then click and order. I don't have to go to a store. I don't have to get in a car. I don't have to move. God, that's heaven."[1]

If you are interested in anything at all—from computers to linens to diamonds to cars—Buy.com, or MySimon.com, or Bloomingdales.com, or productopia.com, or pricecan.com, or any one of hundreds of others, will be happy to assist you. Indeed, if you would like to attend college, or even to get a graduate degree, you may be able to avoid the campus. College education is already being offered on line.[2] A recent advertisement for New York University invites people to attend "the Virtual College at NYU" and emphasizes that with virtual education, you can take a seat "anywhere" in the class—and even sit alone.

It would be foolish to claim that this is bad, or a loss, in general or on balance. On the contrary, the dramatic increase in convenience is a wonderful blessing for consumers. Driving around in search of gifts, for example, can be a real bother. (Can you remember what this used to be like? Is it still like that for you?) For many of us, the chance to point-and-click is an extraordinary improvement. And many people, both rich and poor, take advantage of new technologies to "go" to places that they could not in any sense have visited before— South Africa, Germany, Iran, stores and more stores everywhere, an immense variety of specialized doctors' offices (with some entertaining surprises as you search; for example, lungcancer.com is a law firm's Website, helping you to sue, rather than a doctor's site, helping you to get better). But it is far from foolish to worry that for millions of people, the consequence of this increased convenience is to decrease the set of chance encounters with diverse others—and also to be concerned about the consequence of the decrease for democracy and citizenship.

Or consider the concept of *collaborative filtering*—an intriguing feature on a number of sites, and one that is rapidly becoming routine. Once you order a book from Amazon.com, for example, Amazon.com is in a position to tell you the choices of other people who like that particular book. Once you have ordered a number of books, Amazon.com knows, and will tell you, what other books—and compact discs and movies—you are likely to like based on what people like you have liked. Other Websites, such as Qrate.com and Movie lens, are prepared to tell you which new movies you'll enjoy and which you won't simply by asking you to rate certain movies, then matching your ratings to those of other people, and then finding out what people like you think about movies that you haven't seen. Collaborative filtering is used by CDnow, Moviefinder.com, Firefly, and increasingly many others. We have seen that TiVo, the television recording system, is prepared to tell you what other shows you'll like, based on what shows you now like.

Collaborative filtering is only the beginning. "Personalized shopping" is becoming easily available, and it is intended, in the words of a typical account, to "match the interests and buying habits of its customers, from fabric preferences to room designs to wish lists."[3] Or consider the suggestion that before long we will "have virtual celebrities. . . . They'll look terrific. In fact, they'll look so terrific that their faces will be exactly what *you* think is beautiful and not necessarily what your neighbor thinks, because they'll be customized for each home."[4] (Is it surprising to hear that at least one Website

lots of these curious conditionals

but what is the evidence for that?

provides personalized romance stories? That it asks you for information about "your fantasy lover," and then it designs a story to suit your tastes?)

I'll bet!

In many ways what is happening is quite wonderful, and some of the recommendations from Amazon.com and analogous services are miraculously good, even uncanny. (Thousands of people have discovered new favorite authors through this route.) But it might well be disturbing if the consequence is to encourage people to narrow their horizons, or to cater to their existing tastes rather than to form new ones. Suppose, for example, that people with a certain political conviction find themselves learning about more and more authors with the same view, and thus strengthening their existing judgments, only because most of what they are encouraged to read says the same thing. In a democratic society, might this not be troubling?

The underlying issues here are best approached through two different routes. The first involves an unusual and somewhat exotic constitutional doctrine, based on the idea of the "public forum." The second involves a general constitutional ideal, indeed the most general constitutional ideal of all: that of deliberative democracy. As we will see, a decline in common experiences and a system of individualized filtering might compromise that ideal. As a corrective, we might build on the understandings that lie behind the notion that a free society creates a set of public forums, providing speakers' access to a diverse people, and ensuring in the process that each of us hears a wide range of speakers, spanning many topics and opinions.

THE IDEA OF THE PUBLIC FORUM

In the common understanding, the free speech principle is taken to forbid government from "censoring" speech of which it disapproves. In the standard cases, the government attempts to impose penalties, whether civil or criminal, on political dissent, libelous speech, commercial advertising, or sexually explicit speech. The question is whether the government has a legitimate, and sufficiently weighty, reason for restricting the speech that it seeks to control.

This is indeed what most of the law of free speech is about. But in many free nations, an important part of free speech law takes a quite different form. In the United States, for example, the Supreme Court has ruled that streets and parks must be kept open to the public for expressive activity. In the leading case, from the early part of the twentieth century, the Court said, "Wherever the title of streets and parks may rest, they have immemorially been held in trust for the use of the public and time out of mind, have been used for the purposes of assembly, communicating thought between citizens, and discussing public questions. Such use of the streets and public places has, from ancient times, been a part of the privileges, immunities, rights, and liberties of citizens."[5] Hence governments are obliged to allow speech to occur freely on public streets and in public parks—even if many citizens would prefer to have peace and quiet, and even if it seems irritating to come across protesters and dissidents when you are simply walking home or to the local grocery store.

To be sure, the government is allowed to impose restrictions on the "time, place, and manner" of speech in public places. No one has a right to set off fireworks or to use loudspeakers on the public streets at 3:00 A.M. to complain about global warming or the size of the defense budget. But time, place, and manner restrictions must be both reasonable and limited. Government is essentially obliged to allow speakers, whatever their views, to use public property to convey messages of their choosing.

A distinctive feature of the public forum doctrine is that it creates a *right of speakers' access, both to places and to people.* Another distinctive feature is that the public forum doctrine creates a right, not to avoid governmentally imposed *penalties* on speech, but to ensure government *subsidies* of speech. There is no question that taxpayers are required to support the expressive activity that, under the public forum doctrine, must be permitted on the streets and parks. Indeed, the costs that taxpayers devote to maintaining open streets and parks, from cleaning to maintenance, can be quite high. Thus the public forum represents one area of law in which the right to free speech demands a public subsidy to speakers.

JUST STREETS AND PARKS?
OF AIRPORTS AND THE INTERNET

As a matter of principle, there seems to be good reason to expand the public forum well beyond streets and parks. In the modern era, other places have increasingly come to occupy the role of traditional public forums. The mass media, including the Internet, have become far more important than streets and parks as arenas in which expressive activity occurs.

Nonetheless, the Supreme Court has been wary of expanding the public forum doctrine beyond streets and parks. Perhaps the Court's wariness stems from a belief that once the historical touchstone is abandoned, lines will be extremely hard to draw, and judges will be besieged with requests for rights of access to private and public property. Thus the Court has rejected the seemingly convincing argument that many other places should be seen as public forums. In particular, it has been urged that airports, more than streets and parks, are crucial to reaching a heterogeneous public; airports are places where diverse people congregate and where it is important to have access if you want to speak to large numbers of people. The Court was not convinced, responding that the public forum idea should be understood by reference to historical practices. Airports certainly have not been treated as public forums from "ancient times."[6]

But at the same time, members of the Court have shown considerable uneasiness with a purely historical test. In the most vivid passage on the point, Supreme Court Justice Anthony Kennedy wrote: "Minds are not changed in streets and parks as they once were. To an increasing degree, the more significant interchanges of ideas and shaping of public consciousness occur in mass and electronic media. The extent of public entitlement to participate in those means of communication may be changed as technologies change."[7] What Justice Kennedy is recognizing here is the serious problem of how to "translate" the public forum idea into the modern technological environment. And if the Supreme Court is unwilling to do any such translating, it remains open for Congress and state governments to do exactly that. In other words, the Court may not be prepared to say, as a matter of constitutional law, that the public forum idea extends beyond streets and parks. But even if the Court is unprepared to act, Congress and state governments are permitted to conclude that a free society requires a right to access to areas where many people meet. Indeed, Websites, private rather than public, might reach such conclusions on their own, and take steps to ensure that people are exposed to a diversity of views.

WHY PUBLIC FORUMS? OF ACCESS, UNPLANNED ENCOUNTERS, AND IRRITATIONS

The Supreme Court has given little sense of why, exactly, it is important to ensure that the streets and parks remain open to speakers. This is the question that must be answered if we are to know whether, and how, to understand the relationship of the public forum doctrine to contemporary problems.

We can make some progress here by noticing that the public forum doctrine promotes three important goals.[8] First, it ensures that speakers can have access to a wide array of people. If you want to claim that taxes are too high or that police brutality against African-Americans is widespread, you are able to press this argument on many people who might otherwise fail to hear the message. The diverse people who walk the streets and use the parks are likely to hear speakers' arguments about taxes or the police; they might also learn about the nature and intensity of views held by their fellow citizens. Perhaps some people's views will change because of what they learn; perhaps they will become curious, enough so to investigate the question on their own. It does not much matter if this happens a little or a lot. What is important is that speakers are allowed to press concerns that might otherwise be ignored by their fellow citizens.

On the speakers' side, the public forum doctrine thus creates a right of general access to heterogeneous citizens. On the listeners' side, the public forum creates not exactly a right but an opportunity, if perhaps an unwelcome one: shared exposure to diverse speakers with diverse views and complaints. It is important to emphasize that the exposure is shared. Many people will be simultaneously exposed to the same views and complaints, and they will encounter views and complaints that some of them might have refused to seek out in the first instance. Indeed, the exposure might well be considered, much of the time, irritating or worse.

Second, the public forum doctrine allows speakers not only to have general access to heterogeneous people, but also to specific people and specific institutions with whom they have a complaint. Suppose, for example, that you believe that the state legislature has behaved irresponsibly with respect to crime or health care for children. The public forum ensures that you can make your views heard by legislators, simply by protesting in front of the state legislature itself.

The point applies to private as well as public institutions. If a clothing store is believed to have cheated customers or to have acted in a racist manner, protestors are allowed a form of access to the store itself. This is not because they have a right to trespass on private property—no one has such a right—but because a public street is highly likely to be close by, and a strategically located protest will undoubtedly catch the attention of the store and its customers. Under the public forum doctrine, speakers are thus permitted to have access to particular audiences, and particular listeners cannot easily avoid hearing complaints that are directed against them. In other words, listeners have a sharply limited power of self-insulation.

Third, the public forum doctrine increases the likelihood that people generally will be exposed to a wide variety of people and views. When you go to work or visit a park, it is possible that you will have a range of unexpected encounters, however fleeting or seemingly inconsequential. On your way to the office or when eating lunch in the park, you cannot easily wall yourself off from contentions or conditions that you would not have sought out in advance, or that you would have avoided if you could have. Here too the public forum doctrine tends to ensure a range of experiences that are widely shared—streets and parks are public property—and also a set of exposures to diverse views and conditions. What I mean to suggest is that these exposures help promote understanding and perhaps in a sense freedom. As we will soon see, all of these points can be closely connected to democratic ideals.

We should also distinguish here between exposures that are *unplanned* and exposures that are *unwanted*. In a park, for example, you might encounter a baseball game or a group of people protesting the conduct of the police. These might be unplanned experiences; you did not choose them and you did not foresee them. But once you encounter the game or the protest, you are hardly irritated; you may even be glad to have stumbled across them. By contrast, you might also encounter homeless people or beggars, asking you for money and perhaps trying to sell you something that you really don't want. If you could have "filtered out" these experiences, you would have chosen to do so. For many people, the category of unwanted—as opposed to unplanned—exposures includes a great deal of political activities. You might be bored by those activities, and wish that they were not disturbing your stroll through the street. You might be irritated or angered by such activities, perhaps because they are disturbing your stroll, perhaps because of the content of what is being said, perhaps because of who is saying it.

It is also important to distinguish between exposures to *experiences* and exposures to *arguments*. Public forums make it more likely that people will not be able to wall themselves off from their fellow citizens. People will get a glimpse, at least, of the lives of others, as for example through encountering people from different social classes. Some of the time, however, the public forum doctrine makes it more likely that people will have a sense, however brief, not simply of the experiences but also of the arguments being made by people with a particular point of view. You might encounter written materials, for example, that draw attention to the problem of domestic violence. The most ambitious uses of public forums are designed to alert people to arguments as well as experiences—though the latter sometimes serve as a kind of shorthand reference for the former, as when a picture or a brief encounter has the effect of thousands of words.

In referring to the goals of the public forum doctrine, I aim to approve of encounters that are unwanted as well as unplanned, and also of exposure to experiences as well as

33

arguments. But those who disapprove of unwanted encounters might also agree that unplanned ones are desirable, and those who believe that exposure to arguments is too demanding, or too intrusive, might also appreciate the value, in a heterogeneous society, of exposure to new experiences.

GENERAL INTEREST INTERMEDIARIES AS UNACKNOWLEDGED PUBLIC FORUMS (OF THE WORLD)

Of course there is a limit to how much can be done on streets and in parks. Even in the largest cities, streets and parks are insistently *local*. But many of the social functions of streets and parks, as public forums, are performed by other institutions too. In fact society's general interest intermediaries—newspapers, magazines, television broadcasters—can be understood as public forums of an especially important sort.

The reasons are straightforward. When you read a city newspaper or a national magazine, your eyes will come across a number of articles that you would not have selected in advance. If you are like most people, you will read some of those articles. Perhaps you did not know that you might have an interest in minimum wage legislation, or Somalia, or the latest developments in the Middle East; but a story might catch your attention. What is true for topics is also true for points of view. You might think that you have nothing to learn from someone whose view you abhor. But once you come across the editorial pages, you might well read what they have to say, and you might well benefit from the experience. Perhaps you will be persuaded on one point or another, or informed whether or

not you are persuaded. At the same time, the front page head-
line, or the cover story in *Newsweek*, is likely to have a high
degree of salience for a wide range of people.

Unplanned and unchosen encounters often turn out to do
a great deal of good, both for individuals and for society at
large. In some cases, they even change people's lives. The same
is true, though in a different way, for unwanted encounters. In
some cases, you might be irritated by seeing an editorial from
your least favorite writer. You might wish that the editorial
weren't there. But despite yourself, your curiosity might be
piqued, and you might read it. Perhaps this isn't a lot of fun.
But it might prompt you to reassess your own view and even
to revise it. At the very least, you will have learned what many
of your fellow citizens think and why they think it. What is
true for arguments is also true for topics, as when you encounter, with some displeasure, a series of stories on crime or global
warming or same-sex marriage or alcohol abuse, but find
yourself learning a bit, or more, from what those stories have
to say.

Television broadcasters have similar functions. Maybe the
best example is what has become an institution in many nations: the evening news. If you tune into the evening news,
you will learn about a number of topics that you would not
have chosen in advance. Because of the speed and immediacy
of television, broadcasters perform these public forum–type
functions even more than general interest intermediaries in the
print media. The lead story on the networks is likely to have
a great deal of public saliency, helping to define central issues
and creating a kind of shared focus of attention for many
millions of people. And what happens after the lead story—

dealing with a menu of topics both domestic and international—creates something like a speakers' corner beyond anything ever imagined in Hyde Park.

None of these claims depends on a judgment that general interest intermediaries always do an excellent job, or even a good job. Sometimes such intermediaries fail to provide an adequate understanding of topics or opinions. Sometimes they offer a watered-down version of what most people already think. Sometimes they suffer from prejudices of their own. Sometimes they deal little with substance and veer toward sound bites and sensationalism, properly deplored trends in the last two decades. What matters for present purposes is that in their best forms, general interest intermediaries expose people to a range of topics and views at the same time that they provide shared experiences for a heterogeneous public. Indeed, general interest intermediaries of this sort have large advantages over streets and parks precisely because most of them tend to be so much less local and so much more national, even international. Typically they expose people to questions and problems in other areas, even other nations. They even provide a form of modest, back-door cosmopolitanism, ensuring that many people will learn something about diverse areas of the world, regardless of whether they are much interested, initially or ever, in doing so.

Of course general interest intermediaries are not public forums in the technical sense that the law recognizes. These are private rather than public institutions. Most important, members of the public do not have a legal right of access to them. Individual citizens are not allowed to override the editorial and economic judgments and choices of private owners. In the 1970s, a sharp constitutional debate on precisely this issue resulted in a resounding defeat for those who claimed a constitutionally guaranteed access right.[9] But the question of legal compulsion is really incidental. Society's general interest intermediaries, even without legal compulsion, serve many of the functions of public forums. They promote shared experiences; they expose people to information and views that would not have been selected in advance.

REPUBLICANISM, DELIBERATIVE DEMOCRACY, AND TWO KINDS OF FILTERING

The public forum doctrine is an odd and unusual one, especially insofar as it creates a kind of speakers' access right, subsidized by taxpayers, to people and places. But the doctrine is closely associated with a longstanding constitutional ideal, one that is very far from odd: that of republican self-government.

From the beginning, the U.S. constitutional order was designed to be a republic, as distinguished from a monarchy or a direct democracy. We cannot understand the system of freedom of expression, and the effects of new communications technologies and filtering, without reference to this ideal. It will therefore be worthwhile to spend some space on the concept of a republic, and on the way the American constitution understands this concept, in terms of a deliberative approach to democracy. The general ideal is hardly limited to America; it plays a role in many nations committed to self-government.

In a republic, government is not managed by any king or queen; there is no sovereign operating independently of the

37

people.[10] The American Constitution represents a firm rejection of the monarchical heritage, and the framers self-consciously transferred sovereignty from any monarchy (with the explicit constitutional ban on "titles of nobility") to "We the People." This represents, in Gordon Wood's illuminating phrase, the "radicalism of the American revolution."[11] At the same time, the founders were extremely fearful of popular passions and prejudices, and they did not want government to translate popular desires directly into law. Indeed, they were sympathetic to a form of filtering, though one very different from that emphasized thus far. Rather than seeking to allow people to filter what they would see and hear, they attempted to create institutions that would "filter" popular desires so as to ensure policies that would promote the public good. Thus the structure of political representation, and the system of checks and balances, were designed to create a kind of filter between people and law, so as to ensure that what would emerge would be both reflective and well-informed. At the same time, the founders placed a high premium on the idea of "civic virtue," which required participants in politics to act as citizens dedicated to something other than their self-interest, narrowly conceived.

This form of republicanism involved an attempt to create a "deliberative democracy." In this system, representatives would be accountable to the public at large. But there was also supposed to be a large degree of reflection and debate, both within the citizenry and within government itself.[12] The aspiration to deliberative democracy can be seen in many places in the constitutional design. The system of bicameralism, for example, was intended as a check on insufficiently deliberative action from one or another legislative chamber; the Senate, in particular, was supposed to have a "cooling" effect on popular passions. The long length of service for senators was designed to make deliberation more likely; so too for large election districts. The Electoral College was originally a deliberative body, ensuring that the president would result from some combination of popular will and reflection and exchange on the part of representatives. Most generally, the system of checks and balances had, as its central purpose, the creation of a mechanism for promoting deliberation within the government as a whole.

From these points it should be clear that the Constitution was not rooted in the assumption that direct democracy was the ideal, to be replaced by republican institutions only because direct democracy was impractical in light of what were, by modern standards, extremely primitive technologies for communication. Many recent observers have suggested that, for the first time in the history of the world, something like direct democracy has become feasible. It is now possible for citizens to tell their government, every week if not every day, what they would like it to do.[13] Indeed, Websites have been designed to enable citizens to do precisely that (vote.com is an example). We should expect many more experiments in this direction. But from the standpoint of constitutional ideals, this is nothing to celebrate, indeed it is a grotesque distortion of founding aspirations. It would undermine the deliberative goals of the original design. Ours has never been a direct democracy, and a good democratic system attempts to ensure informed and reflective decisions, not simply snapshots of individual opinions, suitably aggregated.[14]

HOMOGENEITY, HETEROGENEITY,
AND A TALE OF THE FIRST CONGRESS

There were articulate opponents of the original constitutional plan, whose voices have echoed throughout American history; and they spoke in terms that bear directly on the communications revolution. The antifederalists believed that the Constitution was doomed to failure, on the ground that deliberation would not be possible in a large, heterogeneous republic. Following the great political theorist Montesquieu, they urged that public deliberation would be possible only where there was fundamental agreement. Thus Brutus, an eloquent antifederalist critic of the Constitution, insisted, "In a republic, the manners, sentiments, and interests of the people should be similar. If this be not the case, there will be a constant clashing of opinions; and the representatives of one part will be continually striving against those of the other."[15]

It was here that the Constitution's framers made a substantial break with conventional republican thought, focusing on the potential uses of diversity for democratic debate. For them, heterogeneity, far from being an obstacle, would be a creative force, improving deliberation and producing better outcomes. If everyone agreed, what would people need to talk about? Why would they want to talk at all? Alexander Hamilton invoked this point to defend discussion among diverse people within a bicameral legislature, urging, in what could be taken as a direct response to Brutus, that "the jarring of parties . . . will promote deliberation."[16] And in an often forgotten episode in the very first Congress, the nation rejected a proposed part of the original Bill of Rights, a "right" on the part of citizens to "instruct" their representative on how to vote. The proposed right was justified on republican (what we would call democratic) grounds. To many people, it seemed a good way of ensuring accountability on the part of public officials. But the early Congress decided that such a right would be a betrayal of republican principles. Senator Roger Sherman's voice was the clearest and most firm:

> The words are calculated to mislead the people, by conveying an idea that they have a right to control the debates of the Legislature. This cannot be admitted to be just, because it would destroy the object of their meeting. I think, when the people have chosen a representative, it is his duty to meet others from the different parts of the Union, and consult, and agree with them on such acts as are for the general benefit of the whole community. If they were to be guided by instructions, there would be no use in deliberation.[17]

Sherman's words reflect the founders' general receptivity to deliberation among people who are quite diverse and who disagree on issues both large and small. Indeed, it was through deliberation among such persons that "such acts as are for the general benefit of the whole community" would emerge. Of course the framers were not naive. Sometimes some regions, and some groups, would gain while others would lose. What was and remains important is that the resulting pattern of gains and losses would themselves have to be defended by reference to reasons. Indeed, the Constitution might well be seen as intended to create a "republic of reasons" in which the use of govenmental power would have to be justified, not simply supported, by those who asked for it.

We can even take Sherman's conception of the task of the representative as having a corresponding conception of the task of the idealized citizen in a well-functioning republic. Citizens are not supposed to press their self-interest, narrowly conceived, nor are they to insulate themselves from the judgments of others. Even if they are concerned with the public good, they might make errors of fact or of value, errors that can be reduced or corrected through the exchange of ideas. Insofar as people are acting in their capacity as citizens, their duty is to "meet others" and "consult," sometimes through face-to-face discussions or if not through other routes as, for example, by making sure to consider the views of those who think differently.

This is not to say that most people should be devoting most of their time to politics. In a free society, people have a range of things to do. But to the extent that both citizens and representatives are acting on the basis of diverse encounters and experiences, and benefiting from heterogeneity, they are behaving in accordance with the highest ideals of the constitutional design.

E PLURIBUS UNUM, AND JEFFERSON VS. MADISON

Any heterogeneous society faces a risk of fragmentation. This risk has been serious in many periods in American history, most notably during the Civil War, but often in the twentieth century as well. The institutions of the Constitution were intended to diminish the danger, partly by producing a good mix of local and national rule, partly through the system of checks and balances, and partly through the symbol of the Constitution itself. Thus the idea of *e pluribus unum* (from many, one) can be found on ordinary currency, in a brief, frequent reminder of a central constitutional goal.

Consider in this regard the instructive debate between Thomas Jefferson and James Madison about the value of a bill of rights. In the founding era, Madison, the most important force behind the Constitution itself, sharply opposed such a bill, on the ground that it was unnecessary and was likely to sow confusion. Jefferson thought otherwise, and insisted that a bill of rights, enforced by courts, could be a bulwark of liberty. Madison was eventually convinced of this point, but he emphasized a very different consideration: the unifying and educative functions of a bill of rights.

In a letter to Jefferson on October 17, 1788, Madison asked, "What use, then, it may be asked, can a bill of rights serve in popular Government?" His basic answer was that the "political truths declared in that solemn manner acquire by degrees the character of fundamental maxims of free Government, and as they become incorporated with the National sentiment, counteract the impulses of interest and passion."[18] In Madison's view, the Bill of Rights, along with the Constitution itself, would eventually become a source of shared understandings and commitments among extremely diverse people. The example illustrates the founders' belief that for a diverse people to be self-governing, it was essential to provide a range of common experiences.

TWO CONCEPTIONS OF SOVEREIGNTY,
AND HOLMES VS. BRANDEIS

We are now in a position to distinguish between two conceptions of sovereignty. The first involves consumer sovereignty, the idea behind free markets. The second involves political sovereignty, the idea behind free nations. The notion of consumer sovereignty underlies enthusiasm for the "Daily Me"; it is the underpinning of any utopian vision of the unlimited power to filter. Writing in 1995, Bill Gates cheerfully predicted, "Customized information is a natural extension. . . . For your own daily dose of news, you might subscribe to several review services and let a software agent or a human one pick and choose from them to compile your completely customized 'newspaper.' These subscription services, whether human or electronic, will gather information that conforms to a particular philosophy and set of interests."[19] Or recall the first epigraph to this book, Gates's celebratory words in 1999: "When you turn on DirectTV and you step through every channel—well, there's three minutes of your life. When you walk into your living room six years from now, you'll be able to just say what you're interested in, and have the screen help you pick out a video that you care about. It's not going to be 'Let's look at channels 4, 5, and 7.'" This is the principle of consumer sovereignty in action.

The notion of political sovereignty underlies the democratic alternative, which poses a challenge to Gates's vision on the ground that it may well undermine both self-government and freedom, properly conceived. Recall here John Dewey's words: "Majority rule, just as majority rule, is as foolish as its critics charge it with being. But it never is *merely* majority rule. . . . The important consideration is that opportunity be given ideas to speak and to become the possession of the multitude. The essential need is the improvement of the methods and constitution of debate, discussion and persuasion. That is *the* problem of the public."

Consumer sovereignty means that individual consumers are permitted to choose as they wish, subject to the constraints provided by the price system, and also by their current holdings and requirements. This idea plays a significant role in thinking not only about economic markets, but also about both politics and communications. When we talk as if politicians are "selling" a message, and even themselves, we are treating the political domain as a kind of market, subject to the forces of supply and demand. And when we act as if the purpose of a system of communications is to ensure that people can see exactly what they "want," the notion of consumer sovereignty is very much at work.

The idea of political sovereignty stands on different foundations. It does not take individual tastes as fixed or given. It prizes democratic self-government, understood as a requirement of "government by discussion," accompanied by reason-giving in the public domain. Political sovereignty comes with its own distinctive preconditions, and these are violated if government power is not backed by justifications, and represents instead the product of force or simple majority will.

Of course the two conceptions of sovereignty are in potential tension. A commitment to consumer sovereignty may well compromise political sovereignty if, for example, free consumer choices result in insufficient understanding of public problems, or if they make it difficult to have anything like a shared or deliberative culture. We will create serious problems if we confound consumer sovereignty with political sovereignty. If the latter is our governing ideal, for example, we will evaluate the system of free expression partly by seeing whether it promotes democratic goals. If we care only about consumer sovereignty, the only question is whether consumers are getting what they want. The distinction matters for policy as well. If the government takes steps to increase the level of substantive debate on television or in public culture, it might well be undermining consumer sovereignty at the same time that it is promoting democratic self-government.

With respect to the system of freedom of speech, the conflict between consumer sovereignty and political sovereignty can be found in an unexpected place: the great constitutional dissents of Supreme Court Justices Oliver Wendell Holmes and Louis Brandeis. In the early part of the twentieth century, Holmes and Brandeis were the twin heroes of freedom of speech, dissenting, usually together, from Supreme Court decisions allowing the government to regulate political dissent. Sometimes Holmes wrote for the two dissenters; sometimes the author was Brandeis. But the two spoke in quite different terms. Holmes wrote of "free trade on ideas," and treated speech as part of a great political market, with which government could not legitimately interfere. Consider a passage from Holmes' greatest free speech opinion.

When men have realized that time has upset many fighting faiths, they may come to believe even more than they believe the very foundations of their own conduct that the ultimate good desired is better reached by free trade in ideas—that the best test of truth is the power of the thought to get itself accepted in the competition of the market, and that truth is the only ground upon which their wishes safely can be carried out. That at any rate is the theory of our Constitution.[20]

Brandeis's language, in his greatest free speech opinion, was quite different.

Those who won our independence believed that the final end of the state was to make men free to develop their faculties; and that in its government the deliberative forces should prevail over the arbitrary. . . . They believed that . . . without free speech and assembly discussion would be futile; . . . that the greatest menace to freedom is an inert people; that public discussion is a political duty; and that this should be a fundamental principle of the American government.[21]

Note Brandeis's suggestion that the greatest threat to freedom is an "inert people," and his insistence, altogether foreign to Holmes, that public discussion is not only a right but "a political duty." Brandeis sees self-government as something dramatically different from an exercise in consumer sovereignty. On Brandeis's self-consciously republican conception of free speech, unrestricted consumer choice is not an appropriate foundation for policy in a context where the very formation of preferences, and the organizing processes of the democratic order, are at stake.

In fact Brandeis can be taken to have offered a conception of the social role of the idealized citizen. For such a citizen, active engagement in politics, at least some of the time, is an obligation, not just an entitlement. If citizens are "inert," freedom itself is at risk. This does not mean that people have to be thinking about public affairs all or most of the time. But it does mean that each of us has rights and duties as citizens, not simply as consumers. As we will see, active citizen engagement is necessary to promote not only democracy but social well-being too. And in the modern era, one of the most pressing obligations of a citizenry that is not inert is to ensure that "deliberative forces should prevail over the arbitrary." For this to happen, it is indispensable to ensure that the system of communications promotes democratic goals. Those goals emphatically require both unchosen exposures and shared experiences. *What about Holmes? So far you're merely stating an asserted preference.*

REPUBLICANISM WITHOUT NOSTALGIA

These are abstractions; it is time to be more concrete. I will identify three problems in the hypothesized world of perfect filtering. These difficulties would beset any system in which individuals had complete control over their communications universe and exercised that control so as to decrease *a)* shared communications experiences and *b)* exposure to materials that would not have been chosen in advance but that nonetheless are beneficial, both to the person who is exposed to them and to society at large.

The first difficulty involves fragmentation. The problem here comes from the creation of diverse speech communities, whose members make significantly different communications choices. A possible consequence is considerable difficulty in mutual understanding. When society is fragmented in this way, diverse groups will tend to polarize, in a way that can

got proof for that?

breed extremism and even hatred and violence. New technologies, emphatically including the Internet, are dramatically increasing people's ability to hear echoes of their own voices and to wall themselves off from others. An important result is the existence of *cybercascades*—processes of information exchange in which a certain fact or point of view becomes widespread, simply because so many people seem to believe it.

The second difficulty involves a distinctive characteristic of information. Information is a public good in the technical sense that once some person knows something, other people are likely to benefit as well. If you learn about crime in the neighborhood or about the problem of global warming, you will probably tell other people, and they will benefit from what you have learned. In a system in which each person can "customize" his own communications universe, there is a risk that people will make choices that generate too little information, at least to the extent that individual choices are not made with reference to their social benefits. An advantage of a system with general interest intermediaries and with public forums—with broad access by speakers to diverse publics—is that it ensures a kind of social spreading of information. At the same time, an individually filtered speech universe is likely to underproduce what I will call *solidarity goods*—goods whose value increases with the number of people who are consuming them.[22] A presidential debate is a classic example of a solidarity good.

The third and final difficulty has to do with the proper understanding of freedom and the relationship between consumers and citizens. If we believe in consumer sovereignty, and if we celebrate the power to filter, we are likely to think that freedom consists in the satisfaction of private preferences—in an absence of restrictions on individual choices. This is a widely held view about freedom. Indeed, it is a view that underlies much current thinking about free speech. But it is badly misconceived. Freedom consists not simply in preference satisfaction but also in the chance to have preferences and beliefs formed under decent conditions—in the ability to have preferences formed after exposure to a sufficient amount of information, and also to an appropriately wide and diverse range of options. There can be no assurance of freedom in a system committed to the "Daily Me."

and that's what German 2-channel TV didn't give me.

The fewer intermediaries there are, the easier they're subverted

3

fragmentation and cybercascades

There is a discussion group in cyberspace. The group was started two years ago by about a dozen political activists, who were concerned about the increasing public pressure for gun control and the perceived "emasculation" of the Second Amendment (in the group's view, a clear ban on government restrictions on the sale of guns). But the group was also troubled by the growing authority of government, especially the national government, over the lives of ordinary people, and worried as well about the threat to our "European heritage" and to "traditional moral values" that is posed by the increasing social power of African-Americans and "radical feminist women." The group's members were fearful that the Republican and Democratic parties had become weak-willed "twins," unable and unwilling to take on the "special interests" who were threatening to "take away our constitutional liberties." The group called itself the Boston Tea Party.

The members of the Boston Tea Party now number well over four hundred people, who regularly exchange facts and points of view, and who share relevant literature with one another. For a majority of the participants, the discussion group provides most of the information on which they base their judgments about political issues. Over the last two years the Boston Tea Party's concerns have been greatly heightened. Nearly 70 percent of the members carry firearms, some as a result of the group's discussions. Small but vigorous protests have been planned, organized, and carried out in three state capitols. A march on Washington, D.C., is now in the works. Recent discussion has occasionally turned to the need for "self-protection" against the state, through civil disobedience and possibly through selective "strikes" on certain targets in the public and private sectors. The motivation for this discussion is the widely disseminated view that the "FBI and possibly the CIA" are starting to take steps to "dismember" the group. One member has sent bomb-making instructions to all members of the Boston Tea Party. No violence has occurred as yet. But things are unquestionably heading in that direction.

So far as I know, there is no Boston Tea Party. This story is not true. But it is not exactly false. It is a composite based on the many discussion groups and Websites, less and often more extreme, that can be found on the Internet. Discussion groups and Websites of this kind have been around for a number of years. On March 23, 1996, for example, the Terrorist's Handbook was posted on the Internet, including instructions on how to make a bomb (the same bomb, as it happens, as was used in the Oklahoma City bombing, where dozens of federal employees were killed). On the National Rifle Association's "Bullet 'N' Board," a place for discussion of matters of mutual interest, someone calling himself "Warmaster" explained how to make bombs out of ordinary household materials. Warmaster explained, "These simple, powerful bombs are not very well known even though all the materials can be easily obtained by anyone (including minors)." After the Oklahoma City bombing, an anonymous notice was posted not to one but to dozens of Usenet news groups, listing all the materials in the Oklahoma City bomb and exploring ways to improve future bombs. Hundreds of hate groups are now reported to be communicating on the Internet, often about conspiracies and (this will come as no surprise) formulas for making bombs. Members of such groups tend to communicate largely or mostly with one another, feeding their various predilections. The two students who launched the attack in Littleton, Colorado, actually had an Internet site containing details about how to make a bomb. Often such sites receive and spread rumors, many of them false and even paranoid.

Of course these are extreme cases. But they reveal something about the consequences of a fragmented speech market. In a system with robust public forums and general interest intermediaries, self-insulation is more difficult, and people will frequently come across views and materials that they would not have chosen in advance. For diverse citizens, this provides something like a common framework for social experience. "Real-world interactions often force us to deal with diversity, whereas the virtual world may be more homogeneous, not in demographic terms, but in terms of interest and outlook. Place-based communities may be supplanted by interest-based communities."[1] Let us suppose that the communications market continues to become far more fragmented, in exactly the sense prophesied by those who celebrate the "Daily Me," and in a way that invites the continuing emergence of highly specialized Websites and discussion groups of innumerable sorts.

What problems would be created as a result?

FLAVORS AND FILTERS

It is obvious that if there is only one flavor of ice cream or only one kind of toaster, a wide range of people will make the same choice. (Some people will refuse ice cream and some will rely on something other than toasters, but that is another matter.) It is also obvious that as choice is increased, different individuals, and different groups, will make increasingly different choices. This has been the growing pattern with the proliferation of communications options. Consider the celebratory words David Bohnett, founder of geocities.com: "The Internet gives you the opportunity to meet other people who are interested in the same things you are, no matter how specialized, no matter how weird, no matter how big or how small."[2]

The specialization of Websites is obviously important here; so too for the existence of specialized discussion groups of countless kinds. But other technologies are important as well. Consider the World Wide Web Consortium's platform for Internet content selection (PICS), which serves to rate and filter content on the Internet. The authors of PICS hope to put in place a system in which users can filter out materials of any kind, through choosing ratings systems from their preferred sources. Those who seek the ratings of the Conservative

Coalition could use its ratings system, whereas those who prefer the ratings system of the American Civil Liberties Union could use its ratings system. This is merely an illustration of the multiple ways in which new technologies reduce the "friction" of ordinary life and permit people, with increasing ease, to devise a communications universe of their choosing. But this is not only an occasion for celebration.

To see this point, it is necessary to think a bit about why people are likely to engage in filtering. The simplest reason is that people often know, or think they know, what they like and dislike. A friend of mine is interested in Russia; he subscribes to a service that provides him with about two dozen stories about Russia each day. If you are bored by news stories involving Russia, or the Middle East, or if you have no interest in Wall Street, you might turn your mind off when these are discussed; and if you can filter your newpaper or video programming accordingly, it's all the better. And many people like hearing discussions that come from a perspective that they find sympathetic. If you are a Republican, you might prefer a newspaper with a Republican slant, or at least without a Democratic slant. Perhaps you will be most willing to trust "appropriately slanted" stories about the events of the day. Your particular choices are designed to ensure that you can trust what you read. Or maybe you want to insulate yourself from opinions that you find implausible, indefensible, or invidious. Everyone considers some points of view beyond the pale, and we filter those out if this is at all possible. Consider the fact that after people make automobile purchases, they often love to read advertisements for the very car that they have just obtained. The reason is that those advertisements tend to be comforting, because they confirm the wisdom of the decision.

We can make some distinctions here. Members of some groups want to wall themselves off from most or all others simply in order to maintain a degree of comfort and possibly a way of life. Some religious groups self-segregate for this reason. Such groups are tolerant of pluralism and interested largely in self-protection; they do not have ambitions on others. Other groups have a self-conscious "combat mission," seeking to convert others, and their desire to self-segregate is intended to strengthen their members' convictions in order to promote long-term recruitment plans. Political parties sometimes think in these terms, and they often ignore the views of others, except when they hold those views up to ridicule. My own empirical study of political Websites (discussed below) suggests that when links are provided to other Websites, it is often to show how dangerous, or how contemptible, competing views really are.

OVERLOAD, GROUPISM, AND *E PLURIBUS PLURES*

In the face of dramatic recent increases in communications options, there is an omnipresent risk of information overload—too many options, too many topics, too many opinions, a cacophony of voices. Indeed the risk of overload and the need for filtering go hand-in-hand. Bruce Springsteen's music may be timeless, but his 1992 hit, "57 Channels (and Nothin' On)," is hopelessly out of date in light of the number of current programming options, at least if contemporary television is put together with the Internet. (Contradicting Springsteen, TiVo exclaims, "There's always something on TV that you'll like!") Filtering, often in the form of narrowing, is inevitable to avoid overload, to impose some order on an overwhelming number of sources of information.

By itself this is not a problem. But when options are so plentiful, many people will take the opportunity to listen to those points of view that they find most agreeable. For many of us, of course, what matters is that we enjoy what we see or read, or learn from it, and it is not necessary that we are comforted by it. But there is a natural human tendency to make choices, with respect to entertainment and news, that do not disturb our preexisting view of the world. I am not suggesting that cyberspace is a lonely or antisocial domain. In contrast to television, many of the emerging technologies are extraordinarily social, increasing people's capacity to form bonds with individuals and groups that would otherwise have been entirely inaccessible. E-mail and Internet discussion groups provide increasingly remarkable opportunities, not for isolation, but for the creation of new groups and connections. This is the foundation for the concern about the risk of fragmentation. *how to snatch apparent defeat from the jaws of actual victory*

Consider some relevant facts about the current communications market. If you take the ten most highly rated television programs for whites, and then take the ten most highly rated programs for African-Americans, you will find little overlap between them. Indeed, seven of the ten most highly rated programs for African-Americans rank as the very *least* popular programs for whites. Similar divisions can be found on the Internet. Some sites are specifically designed for African-Americans and (it is fair to speculate) are not often consulted by others. American Visions, for example, describes itself as "the magazine of Afro-American culture" and as the biggest, if not the first, "Internet site aimed at African-Americans." Afritech was established primarily "as a forum for black professionals and academics to discuss technical issues." Tony Brown Online is said to be, among other things, "a place where blacks can meet one another." Melanet describes itself as offering "the Uncut Black Experience" focused on "peoples throughout the African Diaspora" and provides a number of services, many of them involving African themes. Of course thousands of Websites, probably millions, are written primarily by and for whites (even if their designers were not self-conscious about this). There are sharp divides along lines of gender as well. Only one site (hotmail.com) can be found on both the list of top sites among women over fifty and the list of top sites among men over fifty. Among girls aged twelve to seventeen, the top entertainment sites in 1998 were Eonline.com, Pathfinder.com, and Titanicmovie.com, whereas the top entertainment sites among boys in the same age group were ESPN.com, Playboy.com, and Song Online.

All this is just the tip of the iceberg. Not surprisingly, people of certain interests and political convictions tend to choose sites and discussion groups that support their convictions. "Because the Internet makes it easier to find like-minded individuals, it can facilitate and strengthen fringe communities that have a common ideology but are dispersed geographically. Thus, particle physicists, Star Trek fans, and members of militia groups have used the Internet to find each other, swap information and stoke each others' passions. In many cases, their heated dialogues might never have reached critical mass as long as geographical separation diluted them to a few parts per million."[3] Many of those with committed views on one or another topic—gun control, abortion, affirmative action—speak mostly with each other. In the mid 1990s, a study found "a bleak vision of democratic discourse on the Web," with only 15 percent of partisan sites offering links to opposing viewpoints.[4] The author concludes that "far from fostering deliberative political discourse, most of the surveyed Websites sought to consolidate speech power and served to balkanize the public forum."[5]

My own study, conducted with Lesley Wexler for this book in June 2000, found the same basic picture. Of a random study of sixty political sites, only nine (15%) provide links to sites of those with opposing views, whereas thirty five (almost 60%) provide links to like-minded sites (see table 3.1).

TABLE 3.1. LINKS TO ALLIES AND ADVERSARIES

Political Orientation	Links to Opposition	No Links to Opposition	Links to Like-Minded Sites	No Links to Like-Minded Sites	Total Number of Sites
Republican	3	7	7	3	10
Democrats	1	11	7	5	12
Conservative	1	20	12	9	21
Liberal	4	13	9	8	17
Total	9	51	35	25	60

One of the most striking facts here is that when links to opposing sites are provided, it is often to show how dangerous, or dumb, or contemptible the views of the adversary really are. Talkleft.com, for example, provides links to several Websites with opposing viewpoints, calling them "Political Sites: The Danger Zone." (There are impressive exceptions. To its credit, the National Organization for Women provides links to Promise Keepers, which it considers an antifeminist organization; the American Conservative Union provides a neutral-sounding set of links to sites of presidential candidates.) Even more striking is the extent to which sites are providing links to like-minded sites. Table 3.1 shows the number of sites that have one or more such links; but in a way it greatly understates what is happening. Several organizations, for example, offer links to dozens or even hundreds of like-minded sites. Consider environmentalhealth.com (a liberal environmental organization with over 200 links), democrats.org/yda (93), dems200.org (69), heritage.org (a conservative group; 93), fundems.com (a liberal group; over 200), and rga.org (a Republican group; 50).

All this is perfectly natural, even reasonable. Those who visit certain sites are probably more likely to want to visit similar sites, and people who create a site with one point of view are unlikely to want to promote their adversaries. Nor is definitive information yet available about the extent to which people who consult sites with one point of view are restricting themselves to like-minded sources of information. But what we now know, about both links and individual behavior, supports the general view that many people are mostly hearing more and louder echoes of their own voices. This may well be damaging from the democratic standpoint.

I do not mean to deny the obvious fact that any system that allows for freedom of choice will create some balkanization of opinion. Long before the advent of the Internet, and in an era of a handful of television stations, people made choices among newspapers and radio stations. Magazines and newspapers, for example, often cater to people with definite interests in certain points of view. Since the early nineteenth century, African-American newspapers have been widely read by African-Americans, and these newspapers offer distinctive coverage of common issues and also make distinctive choices about what issues are important.[6] Whites rarely read such newspapers.

But what is emerging nonetheless counts as a significant change. With a dramatic increase in options, and a greater power to customize, comes a corresponding increase in the range of actual choices, and those choices are likely, in many cases, to match demographic characteristics, preexisting political convictions, or both. Of course this has many advantages; among other things, it will greatly increase the aggregate amount of information, the entertainment value of choices, and the sheer variety of options. But there are problems as well. If diverse groups are seeing and hearing quite different points of view, or focusing on quite different topics, mutual understanding might be difficult, and it might be increasingly hard for people to solve problems that society faces together.

Take some extreme examples. Many Americans now believe that AIDS is a minor problem, one that is diminishing in degree and faced largely by people who have recklessly chosen to take risks. Many other Americans think that AIDS is an extremely serious problem, growing in degree, and fueled by government indifference and perhaps even by deliberate efforts by white doctors to spread the disease within African-

have the before? Is there any indication of reduction of common ground?

American communities. Many Americans fear that certain environmental problems—abandoned hazardous waste sites, genetic engineering of food—are extremely serious and require immediate government action. But others believe that the same problems are imaginative fictions generated by zealots and self-serving politicians. Many Americans think that most welfare recipients are indolent and content to live off of the work of others. On this view, "welfare reform," to be worthy of the name, consists of reduced handouts, a step necessary to encourage people to fend for themselves. But many other Americans believe that welfare recipients generally face severe disadvantages and would be entirely willing to work if decent jobs were available. On this view, "welfare reform," understood as reductions in benefits, is an act of official cruelty.

To say the least, it will be difficult for people, armed with such opposing perspectives, to reach anything like common ground or to make progress on the underlying questions. Consider how these difficulties will increase if people do not know the competing view, consistently avoid speaking with one another, and are unaware how to address competing concerns of fellow citizens.

A BRIEF NOTE ON HATE GROUPS

As noted, there are hundreds of Websites created and run by hate groups and extremist organizations. They appear to be obtaining a large measure of success, at least if we measure this by reference to "hits." My own informal survey shows that several hate groups have had well over one hundred thousand visitors, and in at least one case well over one million. What is also striking is that many extremist organizations and hate groups provide links to one another, and expressly attempt to encourage both recruitment and discussion among like-minded people.

Consider one extremist group, the so-called Unorganized Militia, the armed wing of the Patriot movement, "which believes that the federal government is becoming increasingly dictatorial with its regulatory power over taxes, guns and land use."[7] A crucial factor behind the growth of the Unorganized Militia "has been the use of computer networks," allowing members "to make contact quickly and easily with like-minded individuals to trade information, discuss current conspiracy theories, and organize events."[8] The Unorganized Militia has a large number of Websites, and those sites frequently offer links to related sites. It is clear that Websites are being used to recruit new members, to allow like-minded people to speak with one another, and to reinforce or strengthen existing convictions. It is also clear that the Internet is playing a crucial role in permitting people who would otherwise feel isolated, or who might move on to something else, to band together and to spread rumors, many of them paranoid and hateful.

There are numerous other examples along similar lines. A group naming itself the "White Racial Loyalists" calls on all "White Racial Loyalists to go to chat rooms and debate and recruit with NEW people, post our URL everywhere, as soon as possible."Another site announces that "Our multi-ethnic United States is run by Jews, a 2% minority, who were run out of every country in Europe. . . . Jews control the U.S. media, they hold top positions in the Clinton administration . . . and

63

now these Jews are in control—they used lies spread by the media they run and committed genocide in our name." Table 3.2 gives a brief sense of what is now happening.

TABLE
3.2. LINKS AMONG "HATE SITES"

Site	Links to Like-Minded Sites	Links to Opposition
Adelaide Institute (holocaust revisionism)	16	6
Aggressive Christianity	0	0
All Men Must Die	5	0
Altar of Unholy Blasphemy	11	0
Aryan Nations	28	0
Crosstar (nationalistic)	29	0
David Duke Online	11	0
God Hates Fags	7	3
Islam Monitor	0	12
KKK.com	72	0
Martin Luther King, Jr. (revisionist view of King)	0	0
Misogyny Unlimited	92	1
National Association for the Advancement of White People	0	0
Skinheads of the Racial Holy War	100	0
Stormfront (white nationalism)	60	5
Voice of Freedom (antisemitic)	27	5
Vote for USA (antisemitic)	17	0
White Aryan Resistance	0	0
World Church of the Creator	11	0
Total (19)	14 with; 5 without	6 with; 13 without

Here in particular, the provision of opposition links is designed to produce not discussion but instead fear and contempt. Holocaust denial organizations, for example, describe their adversaries as "exterminationists" or "Holocaust enforcers" and provide links with the evident goal of discrediting them. With respect to like-minded sites, several hate groups have formal linking agreements: "You link to us and we'll link to you." One such site lists nearly one hundred such groups, each with a link, under the title "White Pride World Wide." The listed sites include European Knights of the Ku Klux Klan, German Skin Heads, Aryan Nations, Knights of the Ku Klux Klan, Siegheil88, Skinhead Pride, Intimidation One, SS Enterprises, and White Future.

We can sharpen our understanding here if we attend to the phenomenon of *group polarization.* This phenomenon raises serious questions about any system in which individuals and groups make diverse choices, and many people end up in echo chambers of their own design.

GROUP POLARIZATION IN GENERAL

The term *group polarization* refers to something very simple: *After deliberation, people are likely to move toward a more extreme point in the direction to which the group's members were originally inclined.* With respect to the Internet and new communications technologies, the implication is that groups of like-minded people, engaged in discussion with one another, will end up thinking the same thing that they thought before—but in more extreme form.

Consider some examples of the basic phenomenon, which has been found in over a dozen nations.[9]

- After discussion, a group of moderately pro-feminist women will become more strongly profeminist.[10]
- After discussion, citizens of France become more critical of the United States and its intentions with respect to economic aid.[11]
- After discussion, whites predisposed to show racial prejudice offer more negative responses to the question whether white racism is responsible for conditions faced by African-Americans in American cities.[12]
- After discussion, whites predisposed not to show racial prejudice offer more positive responses to the same question.[13]

The phenomenon of group polarization has conspicuous importance to the communications market, where groups with distinctive identities increasingly engage in within-group discussion. Effects of the kind just described should be expected with the Unorganized Militia and racial hate groups as well as with less extreme organizations of all sorts. If the public is balkanized and if different groups are designing their own preferred communications packages, the consequence will be not merely the same but still more balkanization, as group members move one another toward more extreme points in line with their initial tendencies. At the same time, different deliberating groups, each consisting of like-minded people, will be driven increasingly far apart, simply because most of their discussions are with one another.

Note in particular that even if most of us do not use the power to filter so as to wall ourselves off from other points of view, some or many people will do, and are doing, exactly that.

This is sufficient for polarization to occur, and to cause serious social risks. In general, it is precisely the people most likely to filter out opposing views who most need to hear such views. New technologies, emphatically including the Internet, make it easier for people to hear the opinions of like-minded but otherwise isolated others, and to isolate themselves from competing views. For this reason alone, they are a breeding ground for polarization, and potentially dangerous for both democracy and social peace.

There have been two main explanations for group polarization. Massive evidence now supports both these explanations.

The first explanation emphasizes the role of persuasive arguments. It is based on a simple intuition: Any individual's position on any issue is a function, at least in part, of which arguments seem convincing. If your position is going to move as a result of group discussion, it is likely to move in the direction of the most persuasive position defended within the group, taken as a whole.

If the group's members are already inclined in a certain direction, they will offer a disproportionately large number of arguments going in that same direction, and a disproportionately small number of arguments going the other way. As a result, the consequence of discussion will be to move people further in the direction of their initial inclinations. Thus, for example, a group whose members lean against gun control will, in discussion, provide a wide range of arguments against gun control, and the arguments made for gun control will be both fewer and weaker. The group's members, to the extent that they shift, will shift toward a more extreme position

67

begs the qu'n. It may be a better position, supported by superior arguments

against gun control. And the group as a whole, if a group decision is required, will move not to the median position, but to a more extreme point.

On this account, the central factor behind group polarization is the existence of a *limited argument pool*, one that is skewed (speaking purely descriptively) in a particular direction. It is easy to see how shifts might happen with discussion groups on the Internet (consider a group of Democrats, or Socialists, or members of the Unorganized Militia), and indeed with individuals not engaged in discussion but consulting only ideas (on radio, television, or the World Wide Web) to which they are antecedently inclined. The tendency of such discussion groups, and such consultations, will be to entrench and reinforce preexisting positions—often resulting in extremism.

The second mechanism, involving social comparison, begins with the reasonable suggestion that people want to be perceived favorably by other group members, and also to perceive themselves favorably. Once they hear what others believe, they often adjust their positions in the direction of the dominant position. The German sociologist Elisabeth Noell-Neumann has used this idea as the foundation for a general theory of public opinion, involving a "spiral of silence," in which people with minority positions silence themselves, potentially excising those positions from society over time.[14]

Suppose, for example, that people in a certain group believe that they are sharply opposed to affirmative action, feminism, and gun control, and that they also want to *seem* to be sharply opposed to all these. If they are in a group whose members are also sharply opposed to these things, they might well shift in the direction of even sharper opposition after they see what other group members think. In countless studies, exactly this pattern is observed. Of course people will not shift if they have a clear sense of what they think and are not movable by the opinions of others. But most people, most of the time, are not so fixed in their views.

The point has important implications about the effects of exposure to ideas and claims on television, radio, and the Internet—even in the absence of a chance for interaction. Because group polarization occurs merely on the basis of exposure to the views of others, it is likely to be a common phenomenon in a balkanized speech market. Suppose, for example, that conservatives are visiting conservative Websites; that liberals are visiting liberal Websites; that environmentalists are visiting sites dedicated to establishing the risks of genetic engineering and global warming; that critics of environmentalists are visiting sites dedicated to exposing frauds allegedly perpetrated by environmentalists; that people inclined to racial hatred are visiting sites that express racial hatred. To the extent that these exposures are not complemented by exposure to competing views, group polarization will be the inevitable consequence.

THE ENORMOUS IMPORTANCE OF GROUP IDENTITY

For purposes of understanding modern technologies, a particularly important point has to do with perceptions of identity and group membership. Group polarization will significantly increase if people think of themselves, antecedently or otherwise, as part of a group having a shared identity and a degree of solidarity. If they think of themselves in this way,

so all readers of the Journal get more conservative?

group polarization is both more likely and more extreme.[15] If, for example, a number of people in an Internet discussion group think of themselves as opponents of high taxes, or advocates of animal rights, or critics of the Supreme Court, their discussions are likely to move them in quite extreme directions, simply because they understand each other as part of a common cause. Similar movements should be expected for those who listen to a radio show known to be conservative, or who watch a television program dedicated to traditional religious values or to exposing white racism. Considerable evidence so suggests.[16]

Group identity is important in another way. If you are participating in an Internet discussion group, but you think that other group members are significantly different from you, you are less likely to be moved by what they say. If, for example, other group members are styled "Republicans" and you consider yourself a Democrat, you might not shift at all— even if you would indeed shift, as a result of the same arguments, if you were all styled "voters" or "jurors" or "citizens." Thus a perception of shared group identity will heighten the effect of others' views, whereas a perception of unshared identity, and of relevant differences, will reduce that effect, and possibly even eliminate it.

These findings should not be surprising. Recall that in ordinary cases, group polarization is a product of social influences and limited argument pools. If this is so, it stands to reason that when group members think of one another as similar along a salient dimension, or if some external factor (politics, geography, race, sex) unites them, group polarization will be heightened. If identity is shared, persuasive arguments are likely to be still more persuasive; the identity of those who are making them gives them a kind of credential or boost. And if identity is shared, social influences will have still greater force. People do not like their reputations to suffer in the eyes of those who seem most like them. And if you think that group members are in some relevant sense different from you, their arguments are less likely to be persuasive, and social influences may not operate as much or at all.

GROUP POLARIZATION AND THE INTERNET

Group polarization is unquestionably occurring on the Internet. From the discussion thus far, it seems plain that the Internet is serving, for many, as a breeding ground for extremism, precisely because like-minded people are deliberating with greater ease and frequency with one another, and often without hearing contrary views. Repeated exposure to an extreme position, with the suggestion that many people hold that position, will predictably move those exposed, and likely predisposed, to believe in it. One consequence can be a high degree of fragmentation, as diverse people, not originally fixed in their views and perhaps not so far apart, end up in extremely different places, simply because of what they are reading and viewing. Another consequence can be a high degree of error and confusion.

A number of studies have shown group polarization in Internet-like settings. An especially interesting experiment finds particularly high levels of polarization when group members met relatively anonymously and when group identity was emphasized.[17] From this experiment, it is reasonable to

71

speculate that polarization is highly likely to occur, and to be extreme, under circumstances in which group membership is made salient and people have a high degree of anonymity. These are of course characteristic features of deliberation via the Internet.[18]

Consider in this regard a revealing study not of extremism, but of serious errors within working groups, both face-to-face and more importantly online.[19] The purpose of the study was to see how groups might collaborate to make personnel decisions. Resumes for three candidates, applying for a marketing manager position, were placed before the several groups. The attributes of the candidates were rigged by the experimenters so that one applicant was clearly best matched for the job described. Packets of information were given to subjects, each containing only a subset of information from the resumes, so that each group member had only part of the relevant information. The groups consisted of three people, some operating face-to-face, some operating on-line.

Two results were especially striking. First, group polarization was common, in the sense that groups ended up in a more extreme position in line with members' predeliberation views. Second, almost none of the deliberating groups made what was conspicuously the right choice. The reason is that they failed to share information in a way that would permit the group to make an objective decision. In online groups, the level of mistake was especially high, for the simple reason that members tended to share positive information about the emerging winning candidate and negative information about the losers, while also suppressing negative information about the emerging winner and positive information about the emerging losers. These contributions served to "reinforce the march toward group consensus rather than add complications and fuel debate."[20] In fact this tendency was *twice* as large within the online groups. There is a warning here about the consequences of the Internet for democratic deliberation.

FRAGMENTATION, POLARIZATION, RADIO, AND TELEVISION

An understanding of group polarization casts light on the potential effects not only of the Internet but also of radio and television, at least if stations are numerous and many take a well-defined point of view. Recall that mere exposure to the positions of others creates group polarization. It follows that this effect will be at work for nondeliberating groups, in the form of collections of individuals whose communications choices go in the same direction, and who do not expose themselves to alternative positions. Indeed the same process is likely to occur for newspaper choices. General interest intermediaries have a distinctive role here, by virtue of their effort to present a wide range of topics and views. Polarization is far less likely to occur when such intermediaries dominate the scene. A similar point can be made about the public forum doctrine. When diverse speakers have access to a heterogeneous public, individuals and groups are less likely to be able to insulate themselves from competing positions and concerns. Fragmentation is correspondingly less likely.

Group polarization also raises more general issues about communications policy. Consider the "fairness doctrine," now

Consequences of eliminating the Fairness Doctrine

largely abandoned but once requiring radio and television broadcasters to devote time to public issues and to allow an opportunity for those with opposing views to speak. The latter prong of the doctrine was designed to ensure that listeners would not be exposed to any single view—if one view was covered, the opposing position would have to be allowed a right of access. When the Federal Communications Commission abandoned the fairness doctrine, it did so on the ground that this second prong led broadcasters, much of the time, to avoid controversial issues entirely, and to present views in a way that suggested a bland uniformity. Subsequent research has suggested that the elimination of the fairness doctrine has indeed produced a flowering of controversial substantive programming, frequently expressing extreme views of one kind or another; consider talk radio.[21]

Typically this is regarded as a story of wonderfully successful deregulation. The effects of eliminating the fairness doctrine were precisely what was sought and intended. But from the standpoint of group polarization, the evaluation is far more complicated. On the good side, the existence of diverse pockets of opinion would seem to enrich society's total argument pool, potentially to the benefit of all of us. At the same time, the growth of a wide variety of issues-oriented programming—expressing strong, often extreme views, and appealing to dramatically different groups of listeners and viewers—is likely to create group polarization. All too many people are now exposed largely to louder echoes of their own voices, resulting, on occasion, in misunderstanding and enmity. Perhaps it is better for people to hear fewer controversial views than for them to hear a single such view, stated over and over again. At least there is a risk, in the current situation, that too many people will be insulated from exposure to views that are more moderate, or extreme in another direction, or in any case different from their own.

IS GROUP POLARIZATION BAD?
OF ENCLAVE DELIBERATION

Of course we cannot say, from the mere fact of group polarization, that there has been a movement in the wrong direction. Notwithstanding some of the grotesque examples given here, the more extreme tendency might be better rather than worse. Indeed, group polarization helped fuel many movements of great value—including, for example, the civil rights movement, the antislavery movement, and the movement for sex equality. Each of these movements was extreme in its time, and within-group discussion certainly bred greater extremism; but extremism should not be a word of opprobrium. If greater communications choices produce greater extremism, society may, in many cases, be better off as a result. One reason is that when many different groups are deliberating with one another, society will hear a far wider range of views as a result. Even if the "information diet" of many individuals is homogeneous or insufficiently diverse, society as a whole might have a more richer and fuller set of ideas. This is another side of the general picture of social fragmentation. It suggests some large benefits from pluralism and diversity— benefits even if individuals customize and cluster in groups.

We might define *enclave deliberation* as that form of deliberation that occurs within more or less insulated groups, in which like-minded people speak mostly to one another. The Internet, along with other new communications options, makes it much easier to engage in enclave deliberation. It is obvious that enclave deliberation can be extremely important in a heterogeneous society, not least because members of some groups tend to be especially quiet when participating in broader deliberative bodies. In this light, a special advantage of enclave deliberation is that it promotes the development of positions that would otherwise be invisible, silenced, or squelched in general debate. The efforts of marginalized groups to exclude outsiders, and even of political parties to limit their primaries to party members, might be justified in similar terms. Even if group polarization is at work—perhaps *because* group polarization is at work—enclaves, emphatically including those produced by new technologies, can provide a wide range of social benefits, not least because they greatly enrich the social "argument pool."

The central empirical point here is that in deliberating bodies, high-status members tend to speak more than others, and their ideas are more influential—partly because low-status members lack confidence in their own abilities, and partly because they fear retribution.[22] For example, women's ideas are often less influential and sometimes are "suppressed altogether in mixed-gender groups,"[23] and in ordinary circumstances, cultural minorities have disproportionately little influence on decisions by culturally mixed groups. In light of the inevitable existence of some status-based hierarchies, it makes sense to be receptive to deliberating enclaves in which members of multiple groups may speak with one another and develop their views. The Internet is and will continue to be particularly valuable insofar as it makes this easier.

But there is also a serious danger in such enclaves. The danger is that through the mechanisms of social influence and persuasive arguments, members will move to positions that lack merit but are predictable consequences of the particular circumstances of enclave deliberation. In the extreme case, enclave deliberation may even put social stability at risk. And it is impossible to say, in the abstract, that those who sort themselves into enclaves will generally move in a direction that is desirable for society at large or even for its own members. It is easy to think of examples to the contrary, as, for example, in the rise of Nazism, hate groups, and cults of various sorts.

ENCLAVES AND A PUBLIC SPHERE

Whenever group discussion tends to lead people to more strongly held versions of the same view with which they began, there is legitimate reason for concern. This does not mean that the discussions can or should be regulated. But it does raise questions about the idea that "more speech" is necessarily an adequate remedy for bad speech—especially if many people are inclined and increasingly able to wall themselves off from competing views. In democratic societies, the best response is suggested by the public forum doctrine, whose most fundamental goal is to increase the likelihood that at certain points, there is an exchange of views between enclave members and those who disagree with them. It is total or near-total self-insulation, rather than group deliberation as such, that carries with it the most serious dangers, often in the highly unfortunate (and sometimes literally deadly) combination of extremism with marginality.

To explore some of the advantage of heterogeneity, let us engage in a thought experiment. Imagine a deliberating body consisting not of a subset of like-minded people but of all citizens in the relevant group; this may mean all citizens in a community, a state, a nation, even the world. Imagine that through the magic of the computer, everyone can talk to everyone else. By hypothesis, the argument pool would be very large. It would be limited only to the extent that the set of citizen views was similarly limited. Of course social influences would remain. If you are one of a small minority of people who deny that global warming is a serious problem, you might decide to join the crowd. But when deliberation reveals to people that their private position is different, in relation to the group, from what they thought it was, any shift would be in response to an accurate understanding of all relevant citizens, and not a product of a skewed sample.

This thought experiment does not suggest that a fragmented or balkanized speech market is always bad or that the hypothesized, all-inclusive deliberating body would be ideal. It would be foolish to suggest that all discussion should occur, even as an ideal, with all others. The great benefit of deliberating enclaves is that positions may emerge that otherwise would not, and that deserve to play a larger role both within the enclave and within the heterogeneous public. Properly understood, the case for deliberating enclaves is that they will improve social deliberation, democratic and otherwise, precisely because enclave deliberation is often required for incubating

have they done that so far?
I would say so!

FRAGMENTATION AND CYBERCASCADES

new ideas and perspectives that will add a great deal to public debate. But for these improvements to occur, members must not insulate themselves from competing positions, or at least any such attempts at insulation must not be a prolonged affair. The effects of group polarization thus show that with respect to communications, consumer sovereignty might well produce serious problems for individuals and society at large—and these problems will occur by a kind of iron logic of social interactions.

NO POLARIZATION AND DEPOLARIZATION

Group polarization is a common phenomenon. But in certain circumstances, it can be decreased, increased, or even eliminated. Recall that no shift should be expected from people who are confident that they know what they think, and who are simply not going to be moved by what they hear from other people. If, for example, you are entirely sure of your position with respect to nuclear power—if you are confident not only of your precise view but of the certainty with which you ought to hold it—the positions of other people will not affect you. People of this sort will not shift by virtue of any changes in the communications market.

With artful design of deliberating groups, moreover, it is possible to produce *depolarization*—shifts, within groups, toward the middle of the extremes. Suppose, for example, that a group of twelve people is constructed so as to include six people who have one view and six people who think the opposite—for example, half of the group's members believe that global warming is a serious problem, while the other half think that it is not. If most of the members do not have entirely fixed positions, there is likely to be real movement toward the middle. The persuasive arguments view helps explain why this is so. By hypothesis, the "argument pool" includes an equal number of claims both ways.

There is a valuable lesson about possible uses of communications technologies to produce convergence, and possibly even learning, among people who disagree with one another. If people hear a wide range of arguments, they are likely to be moved in the direction of those who disagree with them, at least if the arguments are reasonable.

CYBERCASCADES: INFORMATION AS WILDFIRE, AND TIPPING POINTS

The phenomenon of group polarization is closely related to the widespread phenomenon of *social cascades*. No discussion of social fragmentation and emerging communications technologies would be complete without an understanding of cascades—above all because they become more likely when information, including false information, can be spread to hundreds, thousands, or even millions by the simple press of a button.

It is obvious that many social groups, both large and small, move rapidly and dramatically in the direction of one or another set of beliefs or actions.[24] These sorts of cascades typically involve the spread of information; in fact they are usually driven by information. Most of us lack direct or entirely reliable information about many matters of importance—whether global warming is a serious problem, whether there is a risk of war in India, whether a lot of sugar is really bad for you, whether Mars really exists and what it is like. If you lack a great deal of private information, you might well rely on information provided by the statements or actions of others. A stylized example: If Joan is unaware whether abandoned toxic waste dumps are in fact hazardous, she may be moved in the direction of fear if Mary thinks that fear is justified. If Joan and Mary both believe that fear is justified, Carl may end up thinking so too, at least if he lacks reliable independent information to the contrary. If Joan, Mary, and Carl believe that abandoned hazardous waste dumps are hazardous, Don will have to have a good deal of confidence to reject their shared conclusion. And if Joan, Mary, Carl, and Don present a united front on the issue, others may well go along.

The example shows how information travels and can become quite widespread and entrenched, even if it is entirely wrong. An illustration is, in fact, the widespread popular belief that abandoned hazardous waste dumps rank among the most serious environmental problems; science does not support that belief, which seems to have spread via cascade.[25] Some cascades are widespread but local; consider the view, with real currency in some African-American communities, that white doctors are responsible for the spread of AIDS among African-Americans. One group may end up believing something and another group the exact opposite, and the reason is the rapid transmission of information within one group but not the other.

It should be obvious that the Internet, with Websites containing information designed for particular groups, greatly

81

increases the likelihood of diverse but inconsistent cascades. "Cybercascades" occur every day. Many of us have been deluged with e-mail involving the need to contact our representatives about some bill or other—only to learn that the bill did not exist and the whole problem was a joke or a fraud. Even more of us have been earnestly warned about the need to take precautions against viruses that do not exist. And many thousands of hours of Internet time have been spent on elaborating paranoid claims about alleged nefarious activities, including murder, on the part of President Clinton. A number of sites and discussion groups spread rumors and conspiracy theories of various sorts. "Electrified by the Internet, suspicions about the crash of TWA Flight 800 were almost instantly transmuted into convictions that it was the result of friendly fire. . . . It was all linked to Whitewater. . . . Ideas become E-mail to be duplicated and duplicated again."[26] In 2000, an e-mail rumor specifically aimed at African Americans alleged that "No Fear" bumper stickers bearing the logo of the sportswear company of the same name really promote a racist organization headed by former Ku Klux Klan Grand Wizard David Duke. (If you're interested in more examples, you might consult http://urbanlegends.about.com, a Website dedicated to widely disseminated falsehoods, many of them spread via the Internet.)

As an especially troublesome example, consider widespread doubts in South Africa, where about 20 percent of the adult population is infected by the AIDS virus, about the connection between HIV and AIDS. South African President Mbeki is a well-known Internet surfer, and he learned the views of the "denialists" after stumbling across one of their

Websites. The views of the "denialists" are not scientifically respectable—but to a nonspecialist, many of the claims on their (many) sites seem quite plausible. At least for a period, President Mbeki both fell victim to a cybercascade and, through his public statements, helped to accelerate one, to the point where many South Africans at serious risk are not convinced about an association between HIV and AIDS. It remains to be seen to what extent this cascade effect will turn out to be literally deadly.

With respect to information in general, there is even a "tipping point" phenomenon, creating a potential for dramatic shifts in opinion. After being presented with new information, people typically have different thresholds for choosing to believe or do something new or different. As the more likely believers, that is people with low thresholds, come to a certain belief or action, people with somewhat higher thresholds then join them, soon producing a significant group in favor of the view in question. At that point, those with still higher thresholds may join, possibly to a point where a critical mass is reached, making large groups, societies, or even nations "tip."[27] The result of this process can be to produce snowball or cascade effects, as large groups of people end up believing something—whether or not that something is true—simply because other people, in the relevant community, seem to believe that it is true.

There is a great deal of experimental evidence of informational cascades, which are easy to induce in the laboratory[28]; real world phenomena also have a great deal to do with cascade effects. Consider, for example, going to college, smoking, participating in protests, voting for third-party candidates, striking, recycling, filing lawsuits, using birth control, rioting, even leaving bad dinner parties.[29] In each of these cases, people are greatly influenced by what others do. Often a tipping point will be reached. The Internet is an obvious breeding ground for cascades, and as a result thousands or even millions of people, consulting sources of a particular kind, will believe something that is quite false.

The good news is that the Internet can operate to debunk false rumors as well as to start them. But at the same time, the opportunity to spread apparently credible information to so many people can induce fear, error, and confusion, in a way that threatens many social goals, including democratic ones. As we have seen, this danger takes on a particular form in a balkanized speech market, as local cascades lead people in dramatically different directions. When this happens, correctives, even via the Internet, may not work, simply because people are not listening to one another.

A CONTRAST: THE DELIBERATIVE OPINION POLL

By way of contrast to fragmentation and cybercascades, consider some work by James Fishkin, a creative political scientist at the University of Texas, who has pioneered a genuine social innovation: the deliberative opinion poll.[30] The basic idea is to ensure that polls are not mere "snapshots" of public opinion. Instead people's views are recorded only after diverse citizens, with different points of view, have actually been brought together to discuss topics with one another. Deliberative opinion polls have now been conducted in several nations, including the United States, England, and Australia. It is even possible for deliberative opinion polls to be conducted on the Internet, and Fishkin has initiated experiments in this direction.

In deliberative opinion polls, Fishkin finds some noteworthy shifts in individual views. But he does not find a systematic tendency toward polarization. In England, for example, deliberation led to reduced interest in using imprisonment as a tool for combating crime.[31] The percentage believing that "sending more offenders to prison" is an effective way to prevent crime decreased from 57 percent to 38 percent; the percentage believing that fewer people should be sent to prison increased from 29 percent to 44 percent; belief in the effectiveness of "stiffer sentences" was reduced from 78 percent to 65 percent.[32] Similar shifts were shown in the direction of greater enthusiasm for procedural rights of defendants and increased willingness to explore alternatives to prison.

In other experiments with the deliberative opinion poll, shifts included a mixture of findings, with deliberation leading larger percentages of individuals to conclude that legal pressures should be increased on fathers for child support (from 70% to 85%) and that welfare and health care should be turned over to the states (from 56% to 66%).[33] To be sure, the effect of deliberation was sometimes to create an increase in the intensity with which people held their preexisting convictions.[34] These findings are consistent with the prediction of group polarization. But this was hardly a uniform pattern. On some questions, deliberation shifted a minority position to a majority position (with, for example, a jump from 36 percent to 57 percent favoring policies making divorce "harder to get").[35]

Fishkin's experiments have some distinctive features. They involve not like-minded people, but diverse groups of citizens engaged in discussion after being presented, by appointed moderators, with various sides of social issues. In many ways these discussions provide a model for civic deliberation, complete with reason-giving and political equality. Of course it can be expensive to transport diverse people to the same place. But new communications technologies make the idea of a deliberative opinion poll and of reasoned discussion among heterogeneous people far more feasible—even if private individuals, in their private capacity, would rarely choose to create deliberating institutions on their own. Indeed, Fishkin is now attempting to create deliberative opinion polls on the Internet. There are many efforts and experiments in this general vein.[36]

Here we can find considerable promise for the future, in the form of discussions among diverse people who exchange reasons and who would not, without new technologies, be able to talk with one another at all. If we are guided by the notion of consumer sovereignty, and if we celebrate unlimited filtering, we will be unable to see why the discussions in the deliberative opinion poll are a great improvement over much of what is now happening on the Internet. In short, republican aspirations sharply diverge from the ideal of consumer sovereignty, seeing television as "just another appliance" and dreaming of a future in which, in Gates's words, "you'll be able to just say what you're interested in, and have the screen help you pick out a video that you care about."

The real questions are what sort of ideals we want to animate our choices, and what kinds of attitudes, and regulation, we want in light of that judgment. And here it is important to say that in themselves, new technologies are not biased in favor of homogeneity and deliberation among like-minded people. Everything depends on what people seek to do with the new opportunities that they have. "I've been in chat rooms where I've observed, for the first time in my life, African-Americans and white supremacists talking to each other. . . . [I]f you go through the threads of the conversation, by the end you'll find there's less animosity than there was at the beginning. It's not pretty sometimes . . . [b]ut here they are online, actually talking to each other."[37] The problem is that this remains an unusual practice.

OF DANGERS AND SOLUTIONS

I hope that I have shown enough to demonstrate that for citizens of a heterogeneous democracy, a fragmented communications market creates considerable dangers. There are dangers for each of us as individuals; constant exposure to one set of views is likely to lead to errors and confusions, sometimes as a result of cybercascades. And to the extent that the process entrenches existing views, spreads falsehood, promotes extremism, and makes people less able to work cooperatively on shared problems, there are dangers for society as a whole.

To emphasize these dangers, it is unnecessary to claim that people do or will receive all of their information from the Internet. There are many sources of information, and some of them will undoubtedly counteract the risks I have discussed. Nor is it necessary to predict that most people will speak only with those who are like-minded. Of course many people will seek out competing views. But when technology makes it easy for people to wall themselves off from others, there are serious risks, for the people involved and for society generally.

To be sure, we do not yet know whether anything can or should be done about fragmentation and excessive self-insulation. I will take up that topic in due course. For purposes of obtaining understanding, few things are more important than to separate the question whether there is a problem from the question whether anything should be done about it. Dangers that cannot be alleviated continue to be dangers. They do not go away if or because we cannot, now or ever, think of decent solutions. It is much easier to think clearly when we appreciate that fact.

social glue
and spreading
information

Some people believe that freedom of speech is a luxury. In their view, poor nations, or nations struggling with social and economic problems, should be trying not to promote democracy, but to ensure material well-being—economic growth and a chance for everyone to have food, clothing, and shelter. This view is badly misconceived. If we understand what is wrong with it, we will have a much better sense of the social role of communications.

For many countries, the most devastating problem of all consists of famines, defined as widespread denial of access to food and, as a result, mass starvation. In the Chinese famine of the late 1950s, for example, about thirty million people died. Is free speech a luxury for nations concerned about famine prevention? Would it be better for such nations to give a high priority not to democracy and free speech, but to ensuring economic development? Actually these are foolish questions. Consider the astonishing finding, by the economist Amartya Sen, that in the history of the world, there has *never* been a famine in a system with a democratic press and free elections.[1] Sen's starting point, which he demonstrates empirically, is that famines are a social product, not an inevitable product of scarcity of food. Whether there will be a famine, as opposed to a mere shortage, depends on people's "entitlements," that is, what they are able to get. Even when food is limited, entitlements can be allocated in such a way as to ensure that no one will starve.

But when will a government take the necessary steps to prevent starvation? The answer depends on that government's own incentives. When there is a democratic system with free speech and a free press, the government faces a great deal of pressure to ensure that people generally have access to food. And where officials are thus pressured, they respond. But a system without democratic elections or a free press is likely to enable government to escape public retribution, and hence not to respond to famines. Government officials will not be exposed, nor will they be at risk of losing their jobs.

Here, then, is a large lesson about the relationship between a well-functioning system of free expression and citizens' well-being. Free speech and free press are not mere luxuries or tastes of the most educated classes; they increase the likelihood that government will actually be serving people's interests. This lesson suggests some of virtues, not only for liberty but also for economic development, of having freedom of speech.[2] And this lesson suggests the immense importance, for liberty and well-being, of the Internet itself, which makes it possible for countless people to learn about social and economic problems, and to ask their governments to respond to what they have learned. It is no accident that tyrannical governments have tried to control access to the Internet, partly in order to wall citizens off from knowledge of other systems, partly to insulate their leaders from scrutiny and criticism. Knowledge is the great ally of both freedom and welfare.

But what may be most interesting for present purposes is the fact that once some people have the relevant knowledge— a famine is actually on the horizon— they confer benefits, in the famine case massive benefits, on others who entirely lack that knowledge. Here cascades can be extremely desirable, and in a well-functioning democracy, the factual reports that actually "stick" turn out to be true. There can be no doubt that many of the people who are protected from starvation and death, as a result of this process, do not themselves choose in advance to learn about famines and related government policies. Many of the beneficiaries of democracy take little if any direct advantage of free media outlets or of democratic elections. But it is not necessary that they do in order for the system to work. When some people know about the coming shortages, they can speak out. The consequence is that famines are averted.

SHARED EXPERIENCES

Thus far I have focused on the social problems that would result from a fragmented communications universe. Let us now turn to two related points. The first involves the social benefits of a situation in which many people, in a heterogeneous nation, have a number of common experiences. The second involves the fact that once one person has information, it tends to spread, and hence to benefit others. A well-functioning system of free expression is much easier to understand with reference to these points.

Many private and public benefits come from shared experiences and knowledge and also from a sense of shared tasks. People are well aware of this, and they act accordingly. People may watch what they watch or do what they do largely because other people are watching or doing the same thing. But when the number of communications options grows dramatically, people will naturally make increasingly diverse choices, and their shared experiences, plentiful in a time of general interest intermediaries, will decrease accordingly. This can erode the kind of social glue that is provided by shared experience, knowledge, and tasks.

Consider in this regard Elihu Katz's recent discussion of Israel's one-channel policy—ensuring, for a long period, that television "controlled by the Broadcasting Authority was the only show in town."[3] From the standpoint of democracy, any such policy obviously seems troublesome. But what is less obvious, and more interesting, is some unintended consequences. Within two years of the inauguration of this policy, Katz suggests, "almost everybody watched almost everything on the one monopolistic channel. . . . Moreover, the shared experience of viewing often made for conversation across ideological lines. . . . [T]he shared central space of television news and public affairs constituted a virtual town meeting." One lesson is that a democracy "may be enhanced, rather than impeded, by gathering its citizens in a single public space set aside for receiving and discussing reliable reports on the issues of the day." It is not necessary to think that a one-channel policy is best, or even tolerable, in order to recognize that shared view-

I disagree. And I know,

ing, providing common experiences for most or all, can be extremely valuable from the democratic point of view.

There is a connected point. Information has a special property. When any one of us learns something, other people, and perhaps many other people, are likely to benefit from what we have learned. If you find out about crime in the neighborhood, or about risks associated with certain foods, others will gain from that knowledge. In a system with general interest intermediaries, many of us come across information from which we may not substantially benefit as individuals, but which we spread to others. Society as a whole is much better off as a result. As we will see, a system in which individuals can design their own communications universe threatens to undermine this salutary process, not only because of the risk of spreading false information via cybercascades, but also because the situation of fragmentation prevents true information from spreading as much as it should.

SOLIDARITY GOODS

Most people understand the importance of common experiences, and many of our practices reflect a firm sense of the point. National holidays, for example, help constitute a nation, by encouraging citizens to think, all at once, about events of shared importance. And they do much more than this. They enable people, in all their diversity, to have some common memories and concerns.

At least this is true in nations where national holidays have a vivid and concrete meaning, as they do, for example, in younger democracies such as South Africa, India, and Israel. In the United States, many national holidays have become mere days off from work, and the precipitating occasion for the day off—President's Day, Memorial Day, Labor Day—has become nearly invisible. This is a serious loss. With the possible exception of July 4th, Martin Luther King, Jr. Day is probably the closest thing to a genuinely substantive national holiday, largely because that celebration involves recent events that can be treated as concrete and meaningful. In other words, the holiday is *about* something. A shared celebration of a holiday with a clear meaning helps to constitute a nation and to bring diverse citizens together.

Such events need not be limited to nations. Consider, as an especially dramatic example, the shared worldwide celebration of the Millennium, welcomed in sequence by China, India, Egypt, France, England, New York, Chicago, and California. In a similar vein, one of the great values of the Olympics is its international quality, allowing people from different countries to form bounds of commonality, both directly through participation by athletes, and indirectly through shared viewing and interest. Of course the Olympics is also a vehicle for crude forms of nationalism. But at its best, the governing ethos is cosmopolitan in spirit.

Communications and the media are of course exceptionally important here. Sometimes millions of people follow an election, a sports event, or the coronation of a new monarch, and many of them do so because of the simultaneous actions of others. In this sense, some of the experiences made possible by modern technologies are *solidarity goods*, in the sense that their value goes up when and because many other people are enjoying or consuming them.[4] The point very much bears on the historic role of both public forums and general interest intermediaries. Street corners and public parks were and remain places where diverse people can congregate and see one another. General interest intermediaries, if they are operating properly, give many people, all at once, a clear sense of social problems and tasks.

Why might these shared experiences be so desirable or important? There are three principal reasons.

1 Simple enjoyment may not be the most important thing, but it is far from irrelevant. Often people like many experiences—including experiences associated with television, radio, and the Internet—simply because those experiences are being shared. Consider a popular movie, the Superbowl, or a presidential debate. For many of us, these are goods that are worth less, and possibly worthless, if many others are not enjoying or purchasing them too. Hence a presidential debate may be worthy of individual attention, for many people, in part because so many other people consider it worthy of individual attention.

2 Sometimes shared experiences help to promote and to ease social interactions, permitting people to speak with one another, and to congregate around a common issue, task, or concern, whether or not they have much in common. In this sense shared experiences provide a form of social glue. They help make it possible for diverse people to believe that they live in the same culture. Indeed they help constitute that shared culture, simply by creating common memories and experiences, and a sense of a common enterprise.

3   A fortunate consequence of shared experiences—in particular many of those produced by general interest intermediaries—is that people who would otherwise see one another as quite unfamiliar, in extreme cases as nearly belonging to a different species, can come instead to regard one another as fellow citizens with shared hopes, goals, and concerns. This is a subjective good—felt and perceived as a good—for those directly involved. But it can be an objective good as well, especially if it leads to cooperative projects of various kinds. When people learn about a disaster faced by fellow citizens, for example, they may respond with financial and other help. The point applies internationally as well as domestically; massive relief efforts are often made possible by virtue of the fact that millions of people learn, all at once, about the relevant need.

Any well-functioning society depends on relationships of trust and reciprocity, in which people see their fellow citizens as potential allies, willing to help, and deserving of help, when help is needed. The level, or stock, of these relationships sometimes goes by the name of "social capital."[5] We might generalize the points made thus far by suggesting that shared experiences, emphatically including those made possible by the system of communications, contribute to desirable relationships among citizens, even strangers. A society without such experiences will inevitably suffer a decline in those relationships.

FEWER SHARED EXPERIENCES

Even in a nation of unlimited communications options, some events will inevitably attract widespread attention. But an increasingly fragmented communications universe will reduce the level of shared experiences, simply as a matter of numbers. When there were only three television networks, much of what appeared on television would have the quality of a genuinely common experience. The lead story on the evening news, for example, would provide a common reference point for many millions of people. This is decreasingly true. In the last thirty years, for example, the three major networks have lost about a third of their audience, or thirty million people. As a result of increased options, the most highly rated show on current network television has fewer viewers than the fifteenth most highly rated show in the typical year in the 1970s.

To the extent that choices and filtering proliferate, it is inevitable that diverse individuals, and diverse groups, will have fewer such reference points. Events that are highly salient to some people will barely register on others' viewscreens. And it is possible that some views and perspectives that seem obvious for many people will, for others, be barely intelligible.

This is far from an unambiguously bad thing. When people are able to make specific choices, they are likely to enjoy what they are seeing or doing. Of course a degree of diversity, with respect to both topics and points of view, is highly desirable. Nor am I suggesting that everyone should be required to watch the same thing. The question does not involve requirements at all. My only claim is that a common set

risk or certainty ?

of frameworks and experiences is valuable for a heterogeneous society, and that a system with limitless options, making
for diverse choices, will compromise some important social
values. If we think, with Justice Brandeis, that a great menace
to freedom is an "inert people," and if we believe that a set of
common experiences promotes active citizenship and mutual
self-understanding, we will be concerned by any developments that greatly reduce those experiences. The ideal of consumer sovereignty makes it hard even to understand this
concern. But from the standpoint of republican ideals, the
concern should lie at the center of any evaluation of the system of communications.

WHAT CONSUMERS MIGHT DO
AND WHAT PRODUCERS MIGHT DO

None of this means that shared experiences will disappear.
Of course people know that such experiences are desirable,
and often they cooperate with one another so that they will
have such experiences. Of course the Internet, and e-mail,
make communication much easier, so that like-minded people
can decide, at once, to do or watch the same thing. In this way
new communications technologies can actually promote
shared experiences, even among people who do not know each
other, or who would not otherwise think of one another as
group members. But even with e-mail and discussion groups,
it can be hard for large numbers of people to coordinate
around a single option, at least when the array of options is
itself extremely large. This point is enough to suggest the basis
for my general concern.

Producers of information also have strong incentives to get people to coordinate around a shared option. They might emphasize, for example, that most people, or most people like you, will be watching a television show dealing with crime in the area or with the difficulty of raising children in an urban environment. Or advertisers might stress the importance, for diverse people, of examining a certain Website, in general or at a specific time. In fact an extremely effective way of getting people to engage in certain conduct is to say that most people, or most people like you, are doing exactly that. In this way, ordinary market forces are likely to diminish the problem.

But they will not eliminate it. To the extent that options are limitless, it is inevitable that producers will have some difficulty in getting people to watch something together, even if people would benefit from this route. It is more likely that diverse groups, defined in demographic, political, or other terms, will occasionally coordinate on agreed-upon alternatives; and this will introduce the various problems associated with fragmentation and group polarization.

INFORMATION AS A PUBLIC GOOD

Thus far I have dealt with the purposes served by ensuring common experiences, many of them made available via the media. There is a related and equally important point. Information is a "public good" in a technical sense used by economists: When one person knows something, others are going to be benefited as well. If you learn that a heat wave is coming or that there is a high risk of criminal assault three blocks away, other people are highly likely to learn these things too. In the terminology of economics, those of us who learn things do not fully "internalize" the benefits of that learning; the benefits amount to "positive externalities" for other people.

In this respect, information has properties in common with environmental protection and national defense. When one person is helped by a program for cleaner air or by a strong military, other people will necessarily be helped as well. It is well known that in circumstances of this kind—when public goods are involved—it is hazardous to rely entirely on individual choices. Acting on their own, those who litter or otherwise pollute are all too likely not to consider the harms they impose on others. Acting on their own, people are all too likely not to contribute to national defense, hoping that others will pick up the slack.

What is true for pollution and national defense is true as well for information. Made solely with reference to the concerns of the individuals involved, private choices will produce too much pollution and too little in the way of national defense or information. When you learn, or do not learn, about the pattern of crime in your city, or about whether global warming is a serious problem, you are unlikely to be thinking about the consequences of your learning, or failure to learn, for other people (except perhaps your immediate family). An implication is that an individual's rational choices, made only with reference to individual self-interest, will produce too little knowledge of public affairs. These are the most conventional cases of "market failure"—addressed, in the context of pollution and national defense, by government programs designed to overcome the predictable problems that would come from relying entirely on individual choices.

That's such a high threshold that your argument becomes irrelevant

No one ever planned this, but if they are working well, general interest intermediaries provide an excellent corrective here. When individuals do not design their communications universe on their own, they are exposed to a great deal of material from which they may not much benefit as individuals, but from which they will be able to help many others. Perhaps you would not ordinarily seek out material about new asthma treatments for children; but once you learn a little bit about them, you might tell your friends whose children have asthma. Perhaps you are not much interested in environmental risks; but once you learn about hazards associated with sports utility vehicles, you might be reinforced in your desire not to buy one, and you might tell people you know about the underlying problems. Every day, in fact, millions of people are beneficiaries of information that they receive only because someone else, who has not sought out that information in advance, happens to learn it.

This is emphatically not an argument that from the point of view of dissemination of information, it would be better to abolish the Internet and cable television, and to rely on a system dominated by a few general interest intermediaries. Nothing could be further from the truth. As we have seen, new technologies dramatically accelerate the spreading of information, true as well as false. General interest intermediaries have interests and biases of their own, and for sheer practical reasons, they cannot provide exposure to all topics and viewpoints. My only suggestion is that insofar as there is a perfect ability to filter, something significant will be lost: a situation in which people, learning something notwithstanding their failure to choose to be exposed to it, end up benefiting

of course, there is a

101

others. Even if an increase in communications options is, with respect to information, a significant gain, this remains a serious loss.

FAMINE AS METAPHOR, AND A CLARIFICATION

Return now to Amartya Sen's finding that famines do not occur in nations with free elections and a democratic press. We should take all this not as an isolated or exotic example limited to poor countries at risk of famine, but as a metaphor for countless situations in which a democratic government averts social problems precisely because political pressure forces it do so. The underlying problems often involve crime, pollution, employment opportunities, health risks, medical advances, political candidates, even corruption.

This point shows that there are serious problems if information is seen as an ordinary consumer product. The simple reason is that in a system in which individuals make choices among innumerable options based only on their private interest, they will fail to learn about topics and views from which they may not much benefit, but from which others would gain a great deal. A system with public forums and general interest intermediaries will help correct the problem. A system of unlimited individual filtering, ensuring against unwanted exposures, may well create it.

All this points to dangers with the power to customize, but the argument should not be misunderstood. The new technology has great potential on these counts as well. If the press is free and the Internet is available, information about a potential or actual famine, or any other problem, can be spread to an entire nation, even to the entire world. What I am offering is not a complaint about the Internet, but an account of the frequently overlooked importance, for a system of free expression, of shared experiences and the provision of information to people who would not have chosen it in advance.

SPREADING INFORMATION

A heterogeneous society benefits from shared experiences, many of them produced by the media. These shared experiences provide a kind of social glue, facilitating efforts to solve shared problems, encouraging people to view one another as fellow citizens, and sometimes helping to ensure responsiveness to genuine problems and needs, even helping to identify them as such. A special virtue of unsought exposures to information is that even if individuals frequently do not gain much from that information, they will tell other people about it, and it is here that the information will prove beneficial. If the role of public forums and general interest intermediaries is diminished, and if good substitutes do not develop, those benefits will be diminished as well, with harmful results for republican ideals.

citizens

The authors of the American Constitution met behind closed doors in Philadelphia during the summer of 1787. When they completed their labors, the American public was, naturally enough, exceedingly curious about what they had done. A large crowd gathered around what is now known as Convention Hall. One of its members asked Benjamin Franklin, as he emerged from the building, "What have you given us?" Franklin's answer was hopeful, or perhaps a challenge: "A republic, if you can keep it." In fact we should see Franklin's remark as a reminder of a continuing obligation. The text of any founding document is likely to be far less important, in maintaining a republic, than the actions and commitments of the nation's citizenry over time.

This suggestion raises questions of its own. What is the relationship between our choices and our freedom? Between citizens and consumers? And how do the answers relate to the question whether, and how, government should deal with people's emerging power to filter speech content?

In this chapter my basic claim is that we should evaluate new communications technologies, including the Internet, by asking how they affect us as citizens, not mostly, and certainly not only, by asking how they affect us as consumers. A central question is whether emerging social practices, including consumption patterns, are promoting or compromising our own highest aspirations. More particularly I make two suggestions, designed to undermine, from a new direction, the idea that consumer sovereignty is the appropriate goal for communications policy.

The first suggestion is that people's preferences do not come from nature or from the sky. They are a product, at least in part, of social circumstances, including existing institutions, available options, and past choices. Prominent among the circumstances that create preferences are markets themselves. "Free marketeers have little to cheer about if all they can claim is that the market is efficient at filling desires that the market itself creates."[1] Unrestricted consumer choices are important, sometimes very important. But they do not exhaust the idea of freedom, and they should not be equated with it.

The second suggestion has to do with the fact that in their capacity as citizens, people often seek policies and goals that diverge from the choices they make in their capacity as consumers. If citizens do this, there is no legitimate objection from the standpoint of freedom—at least if citizens are not using the law to disfavor any particular point of view or otherwise violating rights. Often citizens attempt to promote their highest aspirations through democratic institutions. If the result is to produce a communications market that is different from what individual consumers would seek—if as citizens we produce a market, for example, that promotes exposure to serious issues and a range of shared experiences—freedom will be promoted, not undermined.

The two points are best taken together. Citizens are often aware that their private choices, under a system of limitless options, may lead in unfortunate directions, both for them as individuals and for society at large. They might believe, for example, that their own choices, with respect to television and the Internet, do not promote their own well-being, or that of society as a whole. They might attempt to restructure alternatives and institutions so as to improve the situation.

At the same time, I suggest that even insofar as we are consumers, new purchasing opportunities, made ever more available through the Internet, are far less wonderful than we like to think. The reason is that these opportunities are accelerating the "consumption treadmill," in which we buy more and better goods not because they make us happier or better off but because they help us keep up with others. As citizens, we might well seek to slow down this treadmill, so as to ensure that social resources are devoted, not to keeping up with one another, but to goods and services that really improve our lives.

CHOICES AND CIRCUMSTANCES: THE FORMATION AND DEFORMATION OF PREFERENCES

Many people seem to think that freedom consists in respect for consumption choices, whatever their origins and content. Indeed, this thought appears to underlie enthusiasm for the principle of consumer sovereignty itself. On this view, the central goal of a well-functioning system of free expression is to ensure unrestricted choice. A similar conception of freedom underlies many of the celebrations of emerging communications markets.

It is true that a free society is generally respectful of people's choices. But freedom imposes certain preconditions, ensuring not just respect for choices and the satisfaction of preferences, whatever they happen to be, but also the free formation of desires and beliefs. Most preferences and beliefs do not preexist social institutions; they are formed and shaped by existing arrangements. Much of the time, people develop tastes for what they are used to seeing and experiencing. If you are used to seeing stories about the local sports team, your interest in the local sports team is likely to increase. If news programming deals with a certain topic—say, welfare reform or a current threat of war—your taste for that topic is likely to be strengthened. And when people are deprived of opportunities, they are likely to adapt and to develop preferences and tastes for what little they have. We are entitled to say that the deprivation of opportunities is a deprivation of freedom—even if people have adapted to it and do not want anything more.

Similar points hold for the world of communications. If people are deprived of access to competing views on public issues, and if as a result they lack a taste for those views, they lack freedom, whatever the nature of their preferences and choices. If people are exposed mostly to sensationalistic coverage of the lives of movie stars, or only to sports, or only to left-of-center views, and never to international issues, their preferences will develop accordingly. There is, in an important respect, a problem from the standpoint of freedom itself. This is so even if people are voluntarily choosing the limited fare.

The general idea here—that preferences and beliefs are a product of existing institutions and practices and that the result can be a form of unfreedom, one of the most serious of all—is hardly new. It is a longstanding theme in political and legal thought. Thus Tocqueville wrote of the effects of the institution of slavery on the desires of many slaves themselves: "Plunged in this abyss of wretchedness, the Negro hardly notices his ill fortune; he was reduced to slavery by violence, and the habit of servitude has given him the thoughts and ambitions of a slave; he admires his tyrants even more than he hates them and finds his joy and pride in servile imitation of his oppressors."[2] In the same vein, John Dewey wrote that "social conditions may restrict, distort, and almost prevent the development of individuality." He insisted that we should therefore "take an active interest in the working of social institutions that have a bearing, positive or negative, upon the growth of individuals." For Dewey, a just society "is as much interested in the positive construction of favorable institutions, legal, political, and economic, as it is in the work of removing abuses and overt oppressions."[3] More recently, Robert Frank and Philip Cook have urged that in the communications market, existing "financial incentives strongly favor sensational, lurid and formulaic offerings" and that the resulting structure of rewards is "especially troubling in light of evidence that, beginning in infancy and continuing through life, the things we see and read profoundly alter the kinds of people we become."[4]

Every tyrant knows that it is important, and sometimes possible, not only to constrain people's actions but also to manipulate their desires, partly by making people fearful, partly by putting certain options in an unfavorable light, partly by limiting information. And nontyrannical governments are hardly neutral with respect to preferences and desires. They hope to have citizens who are active rather than passive, curious rather than indifferent, engaged rather than inert. Indeed, the basic institutions of private property and freedom of contract—fundamental to free societies and indeed to freedom of speech—have important effects on the development of preferences themselves. Thus both private property and freedom of contract have long been defended, not on the ground that they are neutral with respect to preferences, but on the ground that they help to form good preferences—by producing an entrepreneurial spirit and by encouraging people to see one another, not as potential enemies, or as members of different ethnic groups, but as potential trading partners.[5] The right to free speech is itself best seen as part of the project of helping to produce an engaged, self-governing citizenry.

LIMITED OPTIONS: OF FOXES AND SOUR GRAPES

When government imposes restrictions on people's opportunities and information, it is likely to undermine freedom not merely by affecting their choices but also by affecting their preferences and desires. Of course this is what concerned Tocqueville and Dewey, and in unfree nations, we can find numerous examples in the area of communications and media policy, as official censorship prevents people from learning about a variety of ideas and possibilities. This was common practice in communist nations, and both China and Singapore have sought to reduce general access to the Internet, partly in an effort to shape both preferences and beliefs. When information is unavailable and when opportunities are shut off, and known to be shut off, people may not end up not wanting them at all.

The social theorist Jon Elster illustrates the point through the old tale of the fox and the sour grapes.[6] The fox does not want the grapes, because he believes them to be sour, but the fox believes them to be sour because they are unavailable, and he adjusts his attitude toward the grapes in a way that takes account of their unavailability. The fox cannot have the grapes, and so he concludes that they are sour and that he doesn't want them. Elster says, quite rightly, that the unavailability of the grapes cannot be justified by reference to the preferences of the fox, when the unavailability of the grapes is the very reason for the preferences of the fox.

Elster's suggestion is that citizens who have been deprived of options may not want the things of which they have been deprived; and the deprivation cannot be justified by reference to the fact that citizens are not asking for these things, when they are not asking *because* they have been deprived of them. In the area of communications and media policy, it follows that a system of few or dramatically limited options—including, for example, an official government news program and nothing else—cannot reasonably be defended, even if there is little or no public demand for further options. The absence of the demand is likely to be a product of the deprivation. It does not justify the deprivation. This point holds with respect to television stations and the Internet as with everything else.

Thus far I have been making arguments for a range of opportunities, even in societies in which people, lacking such opportunities, are not asking for more. Of course the issue is very different in the communications universe that is the main topic of this book—one in which people have countless possibilities from which to choose. But here too social circumstances, including markets, affect preferences, not only the other way around. From the standpoint of citizenship, and freedom as well, problems also emerge when people are choosing alternatives that sharply limit their own horizons.

Preferences are a product not only of the number of options but also of what markets accentuate and of past choices, and those choices can impose constraints of their own. Suppose, for example, that one person's choices have been limited to sports, and lead him to learn little about political issues; that another person focuses only on national issues, because she has no interest in what happens outside American borders; and that still another restricts himself to material that reaffirms his own political convictions. In different ways, each of these person's choices constrains both citizenship and freedom, simply because it dramatically narrows their field of interests and concerns. This is not a claim that people should be required to see things that do not interest them; it is a more mundane point about how any existing market, and our own choices, can limit or expand our freedom.

Indeed people are often aware of this fact, and make choices so as to promote wider understanding and better formation of their own preferences. Sometimes we select radio

still, though: what do you want to do about it?

and television programs and Websites from which we will learn something, even if the programs and the sites we choose are more demanding and less fun than the alternatives. And we may even lament the very choices that we make, on the ground that what we have done, as consumers, does not serve our long-term interests. Whether or not people actually lament their choices, they sometimes have good reason to do so, and they know this without saying so.

These points underlie some of the most important functions of public forums and of general interest intermediaries. Both of these produce unanticipated exposures that help promote the free formation of preferences, even in a world of numerous options. In this sense, they are continuous with the educational system. Indeed they provide a kind of continuing education for adults, something that a free society cannot do without. It does not matter whether the government is directly responsible for the institutions that perform this role. What matters is that they exist.

DEMOCRATIC INSTITUTIONS AND CONSUMER SOVEREIGNTY

None of these points means that some abstraction called "government" should feel free to move preferences and beliefs in what it considers to be desirable directions. The central question is whether citizens in a democratic system, aware of the points made thus far, might want to make choices that diverge from those that they make in their capacity as private consumers. Sometimes this does appear to be their desire. What I am suggesting is that when this is the case, there is, in *oh?*

general, no legitimate objection if government responds. The public's effort to counteract the adverse effects of consumer choices should not be disparaged as a form of government meddling or unacceptable paternalism, at least if the government is democratic and reacting to the reflective judgments of the citizenry.

What we think and what we want often depends on the social role in which we find ourselves, and the role of citizen is very different from the role of consumer. Citizens do not think and act as consumers. Indeed, most citizens have no difficulty in distinguishing between the two. Frequently a nation's political choices could not be understood if viewed only as a process of implementing people's desires in their capacity as consumers. For example, some people support efforts to promote serious coverage of public issues on television, even though their own consumption patterns favor situation comedies; they seek stringent laws protecting the environment or endangered species, even though they do not use the public parks or derive material benefits from protection of such species; they approve of laws calling for social security and welfare even though they do not save or give to the poor; they support antidiscrimination laws even though their own behavior is hardly race- or gender-neutral. The choices people make as political participants seem systematically different from those they make as consumers.

Why is this? Is it a puzzle or a paradox? The most basic answer is that people's behavior as citizens reflects a variety of distinctive influences. In their role as citizens, people might seek to implement their highest aspirations in political behavior when they do not do so in private consumption. They

114

But who are "people as citizens"? Plebiscites? The "State"? Congress? State legislatures?

might aspire to a communications system of a particular kind, one that promotes democratic goals, and they might try to promote that aspiration through law. Acting in the fashion of Ulysses anticipating the Sirens, people might "precommit" themselves, in democratic processes, to a course of action that they consider to be in the general interest. And in their capacity as citizens, they might attempt to satisfy altruistic or other-regarding desires, which diverge from the self-interested preferences often characteristic of the behavior of consumers in markets. In fact social and cultural norms often incline people to express aspirational or altruistic goals more often in political behavior than in markets. Of course selfish behavior is common in politics; but such norms often press people, in their capacity as citizens, in the direction of a concern for others or for the public interest.

Indeed, the deliberative aspects of politics, bringing additional information and perspectives to bear, often affects people's judgments as these are expressed through governmental processes. A principal function of a democratic system is to ensure that through representative or participatory processes, new or submerged voices, or novel depictions of where interests lie and what they in fact are, are heard and understood. If representatives or citizens are able to participate in a collective discussion of broadcasting or the appropriate nature of the Internet, they can generate a far fuller and richer picture of the central social goals, and of how they might be served, than can be provided through individual decisions as registered in the market. It should hardly be surprising if preferences, values, and perceptions of what matters, to individuals and to societies, are changed as a result of that process.

Are you presupposing a mobilized citizenship a la Ackerman?

UNANIMITY AND MAJORITY RULE

Arguments based on citizens' collective desires are irresistible if the measure at issue is adopted unanimously—if all citizens are for it. But more serious difficulties are produced if (as is usual) the law imposes on a minority what it regards as a burden rather than a benefit. Suppose, for example, that a majority wants to require free television time for candidates or to have three hours of educational programming for children each week—but that a minority objects, contending that it is indifferent to speech by candidates, and that it does not care if there is more educational programming for children. Or suppose that in response to the danger of group polarization, a majority wants to require that Websites that propound one political view must provide links to Websites promoting another view. It might be thought that those who perceive a need to bind themselves to a duty, or a course of action of some kind, should not be permitted to do so if the consequence is to bind others who perceive no such need.

Any interference with the preferences of the minority is indeed unfortunate. But in general, it is difficult to see what argument there might be for an across-the-board rule against the modest kind of democratic action that I will be defending here. If the majority is prohibited from promoting its aspirations or vindicating its considered judgments through legislation, people will be less able to engage in democratic self-government. The choice is between the considered judgments of the majority and the preferences of the minority. I am not suggesting, of course, that the minority should be fore-

they exist ? show me !

you assume integrity of process and administration. why?

closed where its rights are genuinely at risk. As we shall see in chapter 8, the remedies that I will suggest do not fall in that category.

UNHAPPY SOVEREIGNS: THE CONSUMPTION TREADMILL

Throughout the discussion I have assumed that insofar as people are indeed acting as consumers, new communications technologies are an unambiguous boon. This is a widespread assumption, and it is easy to see why. If you want to buy anything at all, it has become much easier to do so. If you'd like a Toyota Camry, or a Ford Taurus, or a sports utility vehicle, many sites are available; wallets and watches and wristbands are easily found on-line; shirts and sweaters can be purchased in seconds. Nor is convenience the only point. As a result of the Internet, ordinary people have a much greater range of choices, and competitive pressures are, in a sense, far more intense for producers. Just to take one example, priceline.com allows you to "Name Your Own Price" for airline tickets, hotel rooms, groceries, new cars, mortgages, rental cars, sporting goods, strollers, swings, televisions, exercise equipment, and much more.

Indeed the growth of options for consumers has been a prime engine behind the growth of the Internet. In the early years, the list of the most popular sites was dominated by .edu domains. As late as 1996, no e-commerce sites ranked among the top fifteen. By 1999, the picture had changed in such a way that 1996 traffic patterns had become barely recognizable. In January 1999, the top-ranked .edu site, the University of Michigan, ranked ninety-second. Only three of the fifteen top-ranked sites from January 1996 remained in the top rank three years later (AOL, Netscape, and Yahoo). Commercial enterprises had a substantial presence on the list.

Commercial sites have been growing most rapidly as well, to the point where there were nearly twenty-five million .com sites in January 2000, as compared to six million .edu sites and under one million .gov sites. Consider tables 5.1 and 5.2.

TABLE 5.1. HOW MANY "DOTS"?

Domain	Host Count (January 2000)
.com	24,863,331
.edu	6,085,137
.org	959,827
.gov	777,750

TABLE 5.2.
PERCENTAGE OF .COMS OVER TIME

Date	Number of Websites	.com Sites (percent)
June 1993	130	1.5
December 1993	623	4.6
June 1994	2,738	13.5
December 1994	10,022	18.3
June 1995	23,500	31.3
January 1996	100,000	50
June 1996	230,000 (est.)	68
January 1997	650,000 (est.)	62.6

Insofar as the number of .coms is growing, it might seem clear that consumers, as consumers, are far better off as a result. But there is a problem: Extensive evidence shows that *our experience of many goods and services is largely a product of what other people have, and when there is a general improvement in everyone's consumer goods, people's well-being is increased little or not at all.*[7] Notwithstanding the evidence on its behalf, this might seem to be a positively weird suggestion. Isn't it obvious that better consumer goods are good for consumers? Actually it isn't so obvious. The reason is that people evaluate many goods by seeing how they compare to goods generally. If consumer goods as a whole are (say) 20 percent better, people are not going to be 20 percent happier, and they may not be happier at all.

To see the point, imagine that your current computer is the average computer from ten years ago. Chances are good that ten years ago, that computer was entirely fine, for you as for most other people. Chances are also good that if there had been no advances in computers, and if each of us had the same computer, in terms of quality, as we had ten years ago, little would be amiss. But in light of the massive improvement in computers in the last decade, you would undoubtedly be disappointed by continuing to own a computer from ten years before. Partly this is because it would seem hopelessly slow and infuriatingly inefficient, since the frame of reference has been set by much more advanced computers. Partly this is because your decade-old computer will not be able to interact well with modern ones, and it will place you at a serious disadvantage in dealing with others, not least in the marketplace.

This point need not depend on a claim that people are envious of their neighbors (though sometimes they are), or that people care a great deal about their status and on how they are doing in comparison with others (though status is indeed important). For many goods, the key point, developed by the economist Robert Frank, is that the frame of reference is set socially, not individually.[8] Our experience of what we have is determined by that frame of reference. What the Internet is doing is to alter the frame of reference, and by a large degree. This is not an unmixed blessing for consumers, even if it is a terrific development for many sellers.

To evaluate the Internet's ambiguous effects on consumers, it is necessary only to see a simple point: When millions of consumers simultaneously find themselves with improved opportunities to find goods, they are likely to find themselves of a kind of "treadmill" in which each is continually trying to purchase more and better, simply in order to keep up with others and with the ever-shifting frame of reference. Indeed, what is true for computers is all the more true for countless other goods, including most of the vast array of products available on the Internet, such as sports utility vehicles, CD players, and televisions. Computers are evaluated socially, to be sure, but at least it can be said that fast and efficient ones might genuinely improve our lives, not least by enabling us to improve the operation of our democracy. But for many consumer goods, where the frame of reference is also provided socially, what really matters is how they compare to what other people have, and not how good they are in absolute terms. What would be a wonderful car or television, in one time and place, will seem ridiculously primitive in another.

In sum, the problem with the consumption treadmill, moving ever faster as a result of the Internet, is that despite growing expenditures, and improved goods, the shift in the frame of reference means that consumers are unlikely to be much happier or better off. Even if the Internet is making it far easier for consumers to get better goods, or the same goods at a better price, there is every reason to doubt that this is producing as much of an improvement in life, even for consumers, as we like to think.

This argument should not be misunderstood. Some "goods" actually do improve people's well-being, independently of shifts in the frame of reference. Robert Frank argues that these goods tend to involve "inconspicuous consumption," from which people receive benefits apart from what other people have or do.[9] When people have more leisure time, or when they have a chance to exercise and keep in shape, or when they are able to spend more time with family and friends, their lives are likely to be better, whatever other people are doing. But when what matters is the frame set for social comparison, a society focused on better consumer goods will face a serious problem: People will channel far too many resources into the consumption "treadmill," and far too few into goods that are not subject to the treadmill effect, or that would otherwise be far better for society (such as improved protection against crime or environmental pollution, or assistance for poor people).

For present purposes my conclusions are simple. New technologies unquestionably make purchases easier and more convenient for consumers. To this extent, they do help. But they help far less than we usually think, because they accelerate the consumption treadmill without making life much better for consumers of most goods. If citizens are reflective about their practices and their lives, they are entirely aware of this fact. As citizens, we might well choose to slow down the treadmill, or to ensure that resources that now keep it moving will be devoted to better uses. And insofar as citizens are attempting to accomplish that worthy goal, the idea of liberty should hardly stand in the way.

DEMOCRACY AND PREFERENCES

When people's preferences are a product of excessively limited options, there is a problem from the standpoint of freedom, and we do freedom a grave disservice by insisting on respect for preferences. When options are plentiful, things are much better. But there is also a problem, from the standpoint of freedom, when people's past choices lead to the development of preferences that limit their own horizons and their capacity for citizenship.

My central claim here has been that the citizens of a democratic polity may legitimately seek a communications market that departs from consumer choices, in favor of a system that promotes goals associated with both freedom and democracy. Measures that promote these goals might be favored by a large majority of citizens even if, in their capacity as consumers, they would choose a different course. Consumers are not citizens and it is a large error to conflate the two. One reason for the disparity is that the process of democratic choice often elicits people's aspirations. When we are thinking about what we as a nation should do—rather than what each of us as consumers should buy—we are often led to think of our larger, long-term goals. We may therefore seek to promote a high-quality communications market even if, as consumers, we seek "infotainment." Within the democratic process, we are also able to act as a group, and not limited to our options as individuals. Acting as a group, we are thus in a position to solve various obstacles to dealing properly with issues that we cannot, without great difficulty, solve on our own.

These points obviously bear on a number of questions outside of the area of communications, such as environmental protection and antidiscrimination law. In many contexts, people, acting in their capacity as citizens, favor measures that diverge from the choices they make in their capacity as consumers. Of course it is important to impose constraints, usually in the form of rights, on what political majorities may do under this rationale. But if I am correct, one thing is clear: A system of limitless individual choices, with respect to communications, is not necessarily in the interest of citizenship and self-government. Democratic efforts to reduce the resulting problems ought not to be rejected in freedom's name.

what's
regulation?
a plea

On May 4, 2000, my computer received an odd e-mail, entitled "Love Letter for You." The e-mail contained an attachment. When I opened the e-mail, I learned that the attachment was a love letter. The sender of the e-mail was someone I had never met—as it happens, an employee of Princeton University Press, the assistant to the editor of this very book. I thought I probably should look at this love letter, so I clicked once. But it occurred to me that this might not be a love letter at all, and so I didn't click twice.

I had been sent the Love Bug virus, which infected the world's computers in May 2000. This was a particularly fiendish virus. If you opened it, you received not only a love note but also a special surprise: Your computer would send the same love note to every address in your computer's address book. For many people, this was funny, in a way, but also extremely awful and embarrassing—not least for a law professor finding himself in the position, much worse than uncomfortable, of sending countless unwelcome "love letters" to both students and colleagues.

The Love Bug was capable of many impressive feats. For example, it could delete files. It was apparently capable of mutating, so that many people found themselves, not with love letters, but with notes about Mothers' Day—less intriguing and more innocuous, perhaps, than a love letter, but also capable of mischief, as when an employee at a random company finds himself sending dozens of Mothers' Day notes to friends and colleagues, many of them near-strangers (and not mothers). The Love Bug virus was evidently capable of mutating into, or in any case was shortly followed by, its own apparent cure, with matching attachment: HOW TO PROTECT YOURSELF FROM THE ILOVEYOU BUG! This attachment turned out to be a virus too.

The world-wide costs of the Love Bug went well beyond embarrassment. In Belgium, automatic teller machines were disabled. Throughout Europe, e-mail servers were shut down. Significant costs were imposed on the taxpayers as well— partly because affected computers included those of government, partly because governments all over the world cooperated in enforcement efforts. In London, Parliament was forced to close down its servers, and e-mail systems were crippled in the U.S. Congress. At the U.S. Department of Defense, four classified e-mail systems were corrupted. The ultimate price-tag has been estimated at over $10 billion. Ultimately the U.S. Federal Bureau of Investigation traced the originator of this virus to the Philippines, and as of this writing, arrest and prosecution are expected soon. (Here's one vote for a jail sentence, and not a short one.)

A COMMON VIEW

My discussion thus far has involved the social foundations of a well-functioning system of free expression—what such a system requires if it is to work well. But it would be possible for a critic to respond that government and law have no legitimate role in responding to any problems that might emerge from individual choices. On this view, a free society respects those choices and avoids "regulation," even if what results from free choices is quite undesirable; that is what freedom is all about.

If the claim here is really about freedom, I have already attempted to show what is wrong with it. Freedom should not always be identified with "choices." Of course free societies usually respect free choices. But sometimes choices reflect, and can in fact produce, a lack of freedom. But perhaps the argument is rooted in something else: a general hostility to any form of government regulation. This is of course a pervasive and perhaps growing kind of hostility. A quite common argument is that legal interference with the communications market should be rejected, simply because it is a form of government regulation, and to be disfavored for exactly that reason.

Many people make such an argument about the emerging television market. With the extraordinary growth in the number of channels, they argue, scarcity is no longer a reason for regulation; shouldn't government simply leave the scene? Shouldn't it eliminate regulation altogether? The same argument is being made about the Internet, indeed more forcefully, with the suggestion that it should be taken as a kind of government-free zone. Thus cyberspace activist (and former

The worst argument?
(also 130)

Grateful Dead songwriter) John Perry Barlow produced, in 1996, a well-publicized Declaration of the Independence of Cyberspace, urging, among other things, "Governments of the Industrial World . . . I ask you of the past to leave us alone. You are not welcome among us. You have no sovereignty where we gather. . . . You have no moral right to rule us nor do you possess any methods of enforcement we have true reason to fear."[1]

AN INCOHERENT VIEW: REGULATION, AND LAW, EVERYWHERE

The story of the Love Bug suggests that this argument is quite ridiculous. Could any sensible person support a system in which government was banned from helping to protect against computer viruses? But the story of the Love Bug also suggests something more interesting and more subtle. The real problem is that opposition to government regulation is incoherent.

There is no avoiding "regulation" of the communications market—of television, print media, and the Internet. The question is not whether we will have regulation; it is what kind of regulation we will have. Newspapers and magazines, radio and television stations, and Websites—all of these benefit from government regulation every day. Indeed, a system of regulation-free speech is barely imaginable. Those who complain most bitterly about proposed regulation are often those who most profit, often financially, from current regulation. They depend not only on themselves but also on government

spec. v. general
content v contract/prop
(see 130-31)

and law. What they are complaining about is not regulation as such—they need regulation—but a regulatory regime from which they would benefit less than they do under the current one.

To see the point, begin by considering the actual status of broadcast licensees, in both television and radio, for the last six decades and more. Broadcasters do not have their licenses by nature. Their licenses are emphatically a product of government grants—legally conferred property rights, in the form of monopolies over frequencies, given out for free to ABC, CBS, NBC, and PBS. In the early 1990s, government went so far as to give existing owners a right to produce digital television—what was called, by Senator Dole and many others, a "$70 billion giveaway."

This gift from the public—the grant of property rights via government, in this case for free rather than through auction—is simply the most recent and highly publicized way in which government, and law, are responsible for the rights of those who own and operate radio and television stations. Though we often don't think of them this way, property rights, when conferred by law, are a quintessential form of government regulation. They create power and they limit power. They determine who owns what, and they say who may do what to whom. In the case of radio and television broadcasters, they impose firm limits on others, who may not, under federal law, speak on CBS or NBC unless CBS or NBC allows them to do so. It makes no sense to decry government regulation of television broadcasters when it is government regulation that is responsible for the very system at issue. That system could not exist without a complex regulatory framework from which broadcasters benefit.

Nor is it merely the fact that government created the relevant property rights in the first instance. Government also protects these rights, at taxpayers' expense, via the civil and criminal law, both of which prohibit people from gaining access to what broadcasters "own." If you try to get access to the public via CBS, to appear on its channels without its permission, you will have committed a crime, and the FBI itself is likely to become involved. There is considerable irony in the fact that for many years, broadcasters have complained about government regulation; government regulation is responsible for their rights in the first place. There is a particular irony in broadcasters' vociferous objections to the quite modest public interest requirements that have been imposed on them, in the form of (for example) requirements of educational programming for children, attention to public issues, and an opportunity for diverse views to speak. Of course broadcasters may have some legitimate objections here, at least if they can show that meeting these requirements does little good. But what is not legitimate is for broadcasters to act as if public interest regulation imposes law, and government, where neither existed before. Broadcasters could not exist, in their current form, if not for the fact that law and government are emphatically present. It is law and government that make it possible for them to make money in the first place.[2]

What is true for broadcasters is also true for newspapers and magazines, though here the point is less obvious. Newspapers and magazines also benefit from government regulation through the grant of property rights, again protected at taxpayers' expense. Suppose, for example, that you would like to publish something in the *Washington Post* or in *Time* magazine. Perhaps you believe that one or the other has neglected an important perspective and you would like to fill the gap. If you request publication and are refused, you are entirely out of luck. The most important reason is that the law has created a firm right of exclusion—a legal power to exclude others—and has given this right to both newspapers and magazines. The law is fully prepared to back up that right of exclusion with both civil and criminal safeguards. No less than CBS and ABC, the *Washington Post* and *Time* are beneficiaries of legal regulation, preventing people from saying what they want to say where they want to say it.

Now it may be possible to imagine a world of newspapers and magazines without legal protection of this kind. This would be a world without regulation. But what kind of world would this be? Without the assistance of the law, all sides would be left with a struggle to show superior force. In such a world, people would be able to publish where they wanted if and only if they had the power to insist. Newspapers and magazines would be able to exclude would-be authors so long as they had enough power to do so. Who can know who would win that struggle? (Perhaps you have a gun, or a small private army, and can force the *Washington Post* to publish you at gunpoint.) In our society, access to newspapers and magazines is determined not by power but by legal regulation, allocating and enforcing property rights, and doing all this at public expense.

131

THE CASE OF THE INTERNET:
SOME HISTORICAL NOTES

Despite the widespread claim that the Internet is and should be free of government controls, things are not much different in cyberspace. Here too regulation and government support have been omnipresent. But there are some interesting wrinkles in this context, and they are worth rehearsing here, because they bear on the relationship between regulation and the Internet, and because they are interesting in their own right.

Consider history first. This supposedly government-free zone was a creation not of the private sector but of the national government. Indeed, the private sector was given several chances to move things along, but refused, in a way that shows a remarkable lack of foresight. We are used to hearing tales of the unintended bad consequences of government action. The Internet is an unintended good consequence of government action, by the Department of Defense no less. Beginning in the 1960s, the Advanced Research Project Agency (ARPA) of the Department of Defense created a new computer network, originally called the Arpanet, with the specific purpose of permitting computers to interact with one another, thus allowing defense researchers at various universities to share computing resources. In 1972, hundreds and then thousands of early users began to discover e-mail as a new basis for communication. In the early 1970s, the government sought to sell off the Arpanet to the private sector, contacting AT&T to see if it wanted to take over the system. The company declined, concluding that the Arpanet technology was incompatible with the AT&T network. (So much for the prescience of the private sector.)

Eventually the Arpanet expanded to multiple uses, operating under the auspices of the federal government in the form of the National Science Foundation. In 1984, the Domain Name System (DNS) was introduced. By the late 1980s, a number of new networks emerged, some far more advanced than the Arpanet, and the term "Internet" came to be used for the federally subsidized network consisting of many linked networks running the same protocols. In 1989 and 1990 the Arpanet was disbanded and transferred to regional networks throughout the country. A key innovation came in 1990, when researchers at CERN, the European Laboratory for Particle Physics near Geneva, created the World Wide Web, a multimedia branch of the Internet. CERN researchers attempted to interest private companies in building the World Wide Web, but they declined ("too complicated"), and Tim Berners-Lee, the lead researcher and Web inventor, had to build it on his own.

As hard as it now is to believe, the Internet began to become pervasively commercial only in the early 1990s, in part as a result of the enactment of new legislation removing restrictions on commercial activity. It was during that period that direct government funding was largely withdrawn, but indirect funding and support continues. In 1994, the first cyberbank (First Virtual) opened, and Pizza Hut first offered pizza ordering on its Web page. In 1995, the backbone of the national network was sold to a private consortium of corporations, and the government gave one company the exclusive right to register domain names (you can now buy one for about $70). Originally created by the government, the Internet is now largely free of ongoing federal supervision—with the important exception of guaranteed property rights.

THE CASE OF THE INTERNET: REGULATION AGAIN

Simply because government creates and enforces property rights in cyberspace, the Internet, no less than ordinary physical spaces, remains pervaded by government regulation. This does not mean that government should be permitted to do whatever it wants. But it does mean that the real question is what kind of regulation, not whether to have regulation.

As a result of the Love Bug and other viruses, considerable attention has been given in recent years to the risk and the reality of "cyberterrorism"—not only through e-mail attachments, but also when "hackers" invade Websites to disable them or to post messages of their own choosing. This kind of invasion occurs rarely. Why? A key reason is that it is against the law. A complex framework of state, federal, and international law regulates behavior on the Internet, above all by giving site-owners an entitlement to be free from trespass. These entitlements are created publicly and enforced at public expense. Indeed, an immense amount of taxpayer resources—many millions of dollars, including massive efforts by the Federal Bureau of Investigation—are devoted to the protection of these property rights. And when "cyberterrorism" does occur, everyone knows that the government is going to intervene to protect property rights, in part by ferreting out the relevant lawbreakers, in part by prosecuting them.

If we want, we might decline to call this government "regulation." But this would be a matter of semantics. When government creates and protects rights, and when it forbids people from doing what they want to do, it is regulating within any standard meaning of the term. The Internet is hardly an anarchy or regulation-free. The reason is that governments stand ready to protect those whose property rights are at stake.

In this way the system of rights on the Internet is no different, in principle, from the system of rights elsewhere. But the Internet does present one complication. In ordinary space, it is not really possible, as a practical matter, to conceive of a system of property rights without a large government presence. Such a system would mean that property holders would have to resort to self-help, as through the hiring of private police forces; and for most property owners, including newspapers and magazines, this is not really feasible. But something like it is at least a pragmatic possibility on the Internet. We might think, for example, that government could simply step out of the picture and enable site "owners" to qualify as such only to the extent that they can use their technological capacities to exclude others. In such a system, the Website of Amazon.com would be run and operated by Amazon.com, but it would be free from outsiders only to the extent that the owners of Amazon.com could use technology to maintain their property rights. Amazon.com, in sum, would have a kind of sovereignty as a result of technology, and perhaps it could ensure this sovereignty through technology alone.

Because of current technological capacities, this is not an unimaginable state of affairs. Perhaps many people can protect themselves well enough from cyberterrorists and others, without needing the help of government. But even on the Internet, it would not make much sense to force people to rely on technology alone, in light of the great value of civil and criminal law as an aid to the enjoyment of property rights. In any case this imaginary world of self-help is not the world in which we live. The owners of Websites, no less than the owners of everything else, benefit by government regulation; and without it, they would not really be owners at all.

Perhaps all this seems abstract, but the basic point lies at the very heart of the most fundamental of current debates about Internet policy. Consider, for example, an on-line exchange connected with an Internet symposium in the *American Prospect* (the exchange is available at http://www.prospect.org/controversy/open_source/). Eric S. Raymond, a highly influential developer of open-source software, sharply opposes "government regulation" and endorses "laissez faire" and "voluntary norms founded in enlightened self-interest." Stanford law professor and Internet specialist Lawrence Lessig, writing in very much the same terms as those urged here, responds that "contract law, rightly limited property rights, antitrust law, the breakup of AT&T" are also "regulations" made possible by "governmental policy." Answering Lessig, Raymond is mostly aghast. He acknowledges that he has no disagreement if the term regulation is meant to include "not active coercive intervention but policies which I and hackers in general agree with him are **not** coercive, such as the enforcement of property law and contract rights." But to Raymond, purporting to speak for a large "community consensus," the use of the term *regulation* to include this kind of law reflects a deep confusion in Lessig's "model of the world." "Contract and property law contain no proper names; they formalize an equilibrium of power between equals before the law and are good things; regulation privileges one party designated by law to dictate outcomes by force and is at best a very questionable thing. The one is no more like the other than a handshake is like a fist in the face."

Raymond is stating a widespread view; but the deep confusion is his, not Lessig's. Property law and contract rights are unquestionably "coercive" and entirely "active." These rights do not appear in nature, at least not in terms acceptable for human society. When would-be speakers are subject to a jail sentence for invading property rights, coercion is unquestionably involved. This is not true only for homeless people, whose very status as such is unquestionably a product of law. Even those with open-source software rely heavily on property law—in fact, contract law (through licenses) and copyright law to control what happens to their software. Anyone who is punished for violating the copyright law, or for intruding on the "space" of CBS or a Website owner, is coerced within any reasonable understanding of the term. Nor do contract and property law merely "formalize an equilibrium of power." By conferring rights, they *create* an equilibrium of power—an equilibrium that would not and could not exist without "active" choices by government. In a genuine anarchy, in which everything was left to force, who knows what the equilibrium would look like, with respect to software, on the Internet or anywhere else? Contract law and property law are good, even wonderful things; but to many people much of the time, they are no mere handshake, but much more like "a fist in the face."

REGULATION EVERYWHERE, THANK GOODNESS

None of these points should be taken as an argument against those forms of regulation that establish and guarantee property rights. On the contrary, a well-functioning system of free expression *needs* property rights. Such a system is likely to be much better if the law creates and protects owners of newspapers, magazines, broadcasting stations, and Websites. Property rights make these institutions far more secure and stable and, for precisely this reason, produce much more in the way of speech.

In communist countries, communications outlets were (and are) publicly owned, and all holdings were (and are) subject to governmental reallocation; free speech could not flourish in such an environment. Thus the economist Friedrich Hayek, the greatest critic of socialism in the twentieth century, made precisely the points I have made here about the omnipresence of legal regulation but took them as no challenge to a system rooted in property rights: "In no system that could be rationally defended would the state just do nothing," Hayek argued. "An effective competitive system needs an intelligently designed and continuously adjusted legal framework as much as any other."[3]

Nor does anything I have said suggest that it would be appropriate, or even legitimate, for government to control the content of what appears in newspapers and magazines, by saying, for example, that they must cover presidential elections, or offer dissenting opinions a right of reply. But any objection to such requirements must be based on something other than the suggestion that they would interfere with some law-free zone—that requirements of this sort would introduce a government presence where government had been absent before. Government has been there already, and we are much better off for that. If government is trying to do something new or different, the question is whether what it is trying to do would improve or impair democracy or the system of freedom of speech. That question cannot be resolved by reference to complaints about government regulation as such.

If government is attempting to regulate the Internet, or television in its contemporary form, or some technology that combines or transcends both of these, it makes no sense to say that the attempt should fail because a free society opposes government regulation, or government regulation of speech. No free society opposes that. Government regulation of speech, at least in the form of property rights that shut out would-be speakers, is a pervasive part of a system of freedom that respects, and therefore creates, rights of exclusion for owners of communications outlets.

Here, then, is my plea: When we are discussing possible approaches to the Internet or other new communications technologies, we should never suggest that one route involves government regulation and that another route does not. Statements of this kind produce confusion about what we are now doing and about our real options. And the confusion is far from innocuous. It puts those who are asking how to improve the operation of the speech market at a serious disadvantage.

139

sure, but...

Sper. v general, again

A democratic public should be permitted to discuss the underlying questions openly and pragmatically, and without reference to self-serving myths invoked by those who benefit, every hour of every day, from the exercise of government power on their behalf.

freedom
of speech

Were those responsible for the Love Bug protected by the free speech principle? It would be silly to say that they are. But if this form of speech may be regulated, what are the limits on government's power?

Consider a case involving not e-mail but a Website—a case that is, in many ways, likely to be emblematic of the future. The Website in question had a dramatic name: "The Nuremberg Files." It began, "A coalition of concerned citizens throughout the USA is cooperating in collecting dossiers on abortionists in anticipation that one day we may be able to hold them on trial for crimes against humanity." The site contained a long list of "Alleged Abortionists and Their Accomplices," with the explicit goal of recording "the name of every person working in the baby slaughter business in the United States of America." The list included the names, home addresses, and license plate numbers of many doctors who performed abortions, and also included the names of their spouses and children.

clear & present danger?

So far, perhaps, so good. But three of these doctors had been killed. Whenever a doctor was killed, the Website showed a line drawn through his name. The site also included a set of "wanted posters," Old West–style, with photographs of doctors with the word "Wanted" under each one. A group of doctors brought suit, contending that all this amounted in practice to "a hit list" with death threats and intimidation. The jury awarded them over $100 million in damages.

Did the jury violate the free speech principle? Maybe it did. But if you think so, would you allow a Website to post names and addresses of doctors who performed abortions, with explicit instructions about how and where to kill them? Would you allow a Website to post bomb-making instructions? To post such instructions alongside advice about how and where to use the bombs? As we have seen, there is nothing fanciful about these questions. Dozens of Websites now contain instructions about how to make bombs—though to my knowledge, none of them tells people how and where to use them. If you have no problem with bomb-making instructions on Websites, you might consider another question. Does your understanding of free speech allow people to make unauthorized copies of movies, music, and books, and to give or sell those copies to dozens, thousands, or millions of others?

My basic argument here is that the free speech principle, properly understood, is not an absolute and that it does not bar government from taking steps to ensure that communications markets serve democratic self-government and other important social values. However the hardest questions should be resolved, the government can regulate computer viruses, unauthorized copying, and explicit incitement to engage in criminal acts, at least if the incitement is likely to be effective. It would also be acceptable for government to require television broadcasters to provide educational programming for children on television, as in fact it now does; to mandate free air time for candidates for public office; and on the Internet, to take steps to promote exposure to diverse views (see chapter 8).

This is not the place for a full discussion of constitutional doctrines relating to freedom of expression. But in the process of showing the democratic roots of the system of free expression, I attempt to provide an outline of the basic constitutional principles.[1]

EMERGING WISDOM? TELEVISIONS AS TOASTERS

An emerging view is that the First Amendment to the Constitution requires government to respect consumer sovereignty. Indeed, the First Amendment is often treated as if it incorporates the economic ideal—as if it is based on the view, associated with Bill Gates and many others, that consumer choice is what the system of communications is all about. Although it is foreign to the original conception of the free speech principle, this view can be found in many places in current law.

For one thing, it helps to explain the constitutional protection given to commercial advertising. This protection is exceedingly recent. Until 1976, the consensus within the Supreme Court and the legal culture in general was that the First Amendment did not protect commercial speech at all.[2] Since that time, commercial speech has come to be treated more and

& Kosinski

more like ordinary speech, to the point where Justice Clarence Thomas has even doubted whether the law should distinguish at all between commercial and political speech.[3] To date, Justice Thomas has not prevailed on this count. But the Court's commercial speech decisions often strike down restrictions on advertising, and for that reason, those decisions are best seen as a way of connecting the idea of consumer sovereignty with the First Amendment itself.

Belonging in the same category is the continuing constitutional hostility to campaign finance regulation. The Supreme Court has held that financial expenditures on behalf of political candidates are protected by the free speech principle—and in an act of considerable hubris, the Court has also held that it is illegitimate for government to try to promote political equality by imposing ceilings on permissible expenditures.[4] The inequality that comes from divergences in wealth is not, on the Court's view, a proper subject for political control. Here too an idea of consumer sovereignty seems to be at work. Indeed, the political process itself is being treated as a kind of market, in which citizens are seen as consumers, expressing their will not only through votes and statements but also through expenditures.

Even more relevant for present purposes is the widespread suggestion, with some support in current constitutional law, that the free speech principle forbids government from interfering with the communications market by, for example, attempting to draw people's attention to serious issues or regulating the content of what appears on broadcast networks.[5] To be sure, everyone agrees that the government is permitted to create and protect property rights, even if this means that speech will be regulated as a result. We have seen that the government may give property rights to Websites and broadcasters; there is no constitutional problem with that. Everyone also agrees that the government is permitted to control monopolistic behavior and thus to enforce antitrust law, designed to ensure genuinely free markets in communications. Structural regulation, not involving direct control of speech but intended to make sure that the market works well, is also unobjectionable. Hence government can create copyright law and forbid unauthorized copying. But if government attempts to require television broadcasters to cover public issues, or to provide free air time for candidates, or to ensure a certain level of high-quality programming for children, many people will claim that the First Amendment is being violated. The same is true for government efforts to improve the operation of the Internet by, for example, enlisting the public forum doctrine so as to promote exposure to materials that people would not have chosen in advance—a suggestion that I will later develop in more detail.

TWO FREE SPEECH PRINCIPLES

We might distinguish here between the free speech principle as it operates in courts and the free speech principle as it operates in public debate. As far as courts are concerned, there is as yet no clear answer to many of the constitutional questions that would be raised by government efforts to make the speech market work better. For example, we do not really know, as a matter of constitutional law, whether government can require educational and public affairs programming on

145

television. The Supreme Court allowed such regulation when three or four television stations dominated the scene; but it has left open the question whether such regulation would be legitimate today.[6] As a matter of prediction, the most that can be said is that there is a good chance that the Court would permit government to do a great deal, so long as it was promoting goals associated with deliberative democracy.

Indeed the Court has been very cautious, and self-consciously so, about laying down firm rules governing the role of the free speech principle on new technologies. The Court is aware that things are changing rapidly and that there is much that it does not know. Because issues of fact and value are in a state of flux, the Court has tended to offer narrow, case-specific rulings that offer little guidance, and constraint, for the future.[7]

But the free speech principle has an independent life outside of the courtroom. It is often invoked, often strategically though sometimes as a matter of principle, in such a way as to discourage government initiatives that might make the communications market serve republican goals. Outside of the law, and inside the offices of lobbyists and newspapers and even in ordinary households, the First Amendment has a large *cultural* presence. This is no less important than its technical role in courts. Here the identification of the free speech principle with consumer sovereignty is becoming all the tighter. Worst of all, the emerging cultural understanding severs the link between the First Amendment and democratic self-rule.

Recall here Bill Gates's words: "It's already getting a little unwieldy. When you turn on DirectTV and you step through every channel—well, there's three minutes of your life. When you walk into your living room six years from now, you'll be able to just say what you're interested in, and have the screen help you pick out a video that you care about. It's not going to be 'Let's look at channels 4, 5, and 7.'" Taken to its logical extreme, the emerging wisdom would identify the First Amendment with the dream of unlimited consumer sovereignty with respect to speech. It would see the First Amendment in precisely Gates's terms. It would transform the First Amendment into a constitutional guarantee of consumer sovereignty in the domain of communications.

I have had some experience with the conception of the First Amendment as an embodiment of consumer sovereignty, and it may be useful to offer a brief account of that experience. From 1997 to 1998, I served on the President's Advisory Committee on the Public Interest Obligations of Digital Television Broadcasters. Our task was to consider whether and how television broadcasters should be required to promote public interest goals, through, for example, closed captioning for the hearing-impaired, emergency warnings, educational programming for children, and free airtime for candidates. About half of the committee's members were broadcasters, and most of them were entirely happy to challenge proposed government regulation as intrusive and indefensible. One of the two co-chairs was the redoubtable Leslie Moonves, President of CBS. Moonves is an obviously intelligent, public-spirited man, but he is also the furthest thing from a shrinking violet; and Moonves is, to say the least, attuned to the economic interests of the television networks. Because of its composition, this group was not about to recommend anything dramatic. On the contrary, it was bound to be highly

147

respectful of the prerogatives of television broadcasters. In any case the Advisory Committee was just that—an advisory committee—and we had power only to write a report, and no authority to impose any duties on anyone at all.

Nonetheless, the committee was subject to a sustained, intense, high-profile, and extraordinarily well-funded lobbying effort by economic interests, generally associated with the broadcasting industry, seeking to invoke the First Amendment to suggest that any and all public interest obligations should and would be found unconstitutional. A high-priced Washington lawyer testified before us for an endless hour, making quite outlandish claims about the meaning of the First Amendment. A long stream of legal documents was generated and sent to all of us, most of them arguing that (for example) a requirement of free airtime for candidates would offend the Constitution. At our meetings, the most obvious (omni)presence was Jack Goodman, the lawyer for the National Association of Broadcasters (NAB), the lobbying and litigating arm of the broadcast industry, which wields the First Amendment as a kind of protectionist weapon against almost everything that government tries to do. To say that Goodman and the NAB would invoke the free speech principle at the drop of a hat, or the faintest step of a Federal Communications Commission official in the distance, is only a slight exaggeration.

Of course all this was a legitimate exercise of free speech. But when the President's Advisory Committee on the Public Interest Obligations of Digital Television Broadcasters already consists, in large part, of broadcasters, and when that very committee is besieged with tendentious and implausible

cheap shot. Also, the NRA is right

interpretations of the First Amendment, something does seem amiss. There is a more general point. The NAB and others with similar economic interests typically use the First Amendment in precisely the same way that the National Rifle Association (NRA) uses the Second Amendment. We should think of the two camps as jurisprudential twins. The NAB is prepared to make self-serving and outlandish claims about the First Amendment, before the public and before courts, and to pay lawyers and publicists a lot of money to help establish those claims. (Perhaps they will ultimately succeed.) The NRA does the same thing with the Second Amendment. In both cases, those whose social and economic interests are at stake are prepared to use the Constitution, however implausibly invoked, to give a veneer of principle and respectability to arguments that would otherwise seem hopelessly partisan and self interested.

Indeed our advisory committee heard a great deal about the First Amendment, and about marginally relevant Supreme Court decisions, and about footnotes from lower court opinions, but exceedingly little, in fact close to nothing, about the pragmatic and empirical issues on which many of our inquiries should have turned. If educational programming for children is required on CBS, NBC, and ABC, how many children will end up watching? What would they watch, or do, instead? Would educational programming help them? When educational programming is required, how much do the networks lose in dollars, and who pays the tab—advertisers, consumers, network employees, or someone else? What would be the real-world effects, on citizens and fund-raising alike, of free air time for candidates? Would such a requirement produce more

149

good

ok y more

substantial attention to serious issues? Would it reduce current pressures to raise money? What are the consequences of violence on television, for both children and adults? Does television violence actually increase violence in the real world? Does it make children anxious, in a way that creates genuine psychological harm? How, exactly, are the hard-of-hearing affected when captions are absent?

We can go further still. In the early part of the twentieth century, the due process clause of the Fourteenth Amendment was used to forbid government from regulating the labor market through, for example, minimum wage and maximum hour legislation.[8] The Court thought that the Constitution allowed workers and employers to see wages and hours as they "chose," without regulatory constraints. This is one of the most notorious periods in the history of the Supreme Court. Judicial use of the Fourteenth Amendment for these purposes is now almost universally agreed to have been a grotesque abuse of power. Nearly everyone now sees that the underlying questions were democratic ones, not for the judiciary. The Court should not have forbidden democratic experimentation that would, plausibly if not certainly, have done considerable good.

In fact a central animating idea, in these now-discredited decisions, was that of consumer sovereignty—ensuring that government would not "interfere" with the terms produced by workers, employers, and consumers. But in the early part of the twenty-first century, the First Amendment is serving a similar purpose, in popular debate and sometimes in courts as well. All too often, it is being invoked on behalf of consumer sovereignty and to prevent the democratic process from resolving complex questions that turn on issues of fact and value that are ill-suited to judicial resolution. To say this is not to say that the First Amendment should play no role at all. But it is to say that many imaginable initiatives, responding to the problems I have discussed thus far, are fully consistent with the free speech guarantee. Indeed, they would promote its highest aspirations.

FREE SPEECH IS NOT AN ABSOLUTE

We can identify some flaws in the emerging view of the First Amendment by investigating the idea that the free speech guarantee is "an absolute," in the specific sense that government may not regulate speech at all. This view plays a large role in public debate, and in some ways it is a salutary myth. Certainly the idea that the First Amendment is "an absolute" helps to discourage government from doing things that it ought not to do. At the same time it gives greater rhetorical power to critics of illegitimate government censorship. But a myth, even if in some ways salutary, remains a myth, and any publicly influential myth is likely to create many problems.

There should be no ambiguity on the point: Free speech is not an absolute. We have seen that the government is allowed to regulate speech by imposing neutral rules of property law, telling would-be speakers that they may not have access to certain speech outlets. But this is only the beginning. Government is permitted to regulate computer viruses; unauthorized copying of copyrighted works; unlicensed medical advice; attempted bribery; perjury; criminal conspiracies ("let's fix prices!"); threats to assassinate the President; blackmail ("I'll

deliberate overstatement. Straw man.
Black, Douglas & Meiklejohn didn't believe this

tell everyone the truth about your private life unless you give me $100"); criminal solicitation ("might you help me rob this bank?"); child pornography; false advertising; purely verbal fraud ("this stock is worth $100,000"); and much more. Many of these forms of speech will not be especially harmful. A fruitless and doomed attempt to solicit someone to commit a crime, for example, is still criminal solicitation; a pitifully executed attempt at fraud is still fraud; sending a computer virus that doesn't actually work is still against the law. Perhaps you disagree with the view, settled as a matter of current American law (and so settled in most other nations as well), that *all* of these forms of speech are unprotected by the free speech principle. But you are not a free speech absolutist unless you believe that *each* of these forms of speech should be protected by that principle. And if this is your belief, you are a most unusual person (and you will have a lot of explaining to do).

This is not the place for a full account of the reach of the First Amendment of the American Constitution.[9] But it is plain that some distinctions must be made between different kinds of speech. It is important, for example, to distinguish between speech that can be shown to be quite harmful and speech that seems relatively harmless. As a general rule, the government should not be able to regulate the latter. We might also distinguish between speech that bears on democratic self-government and speech that does not; certainly an especially severe burden should be placed on any government efforts to regulate political speech. Less simply, we might want to distinguish among the *kinds of lines* that govern-

"absolutists"

ment is drawing in terms of the likelihood that government is acting on the basis of illegitimate reasons (a point to which I will return).

These ideas could be combined in various ways, and indeed the fabric of modern free speech law in the United States reflects one such combination. Despite the increasing prominence of the idea that the free speech principle requires unrestricted choices by individual consumers, the Supreme Court continues to say that political speech receives the highest protection, and that government may regulate (for example) commercial advertising, obscenity, and libel of ordinary people without meeting the especially stringent burden of justification required for political speech. But for present purposes, all that is necessary is to say that no one really believes that the free speech principle or the First Amendment is an absolute. We should be very thankful for that.

THE FIRST AMENDMENT AND DEMOCRATIC DELIBERATION

The fundamental concern of this book is to see how unlimited consumer options might compromise the preconditions of a system of freedom of expression, which include unchosen exposures and shared experiences. To understand how government should respond to that concern, we will make most progress if we insist that the free speech principle should be read in light of the commitment to democratic deliberation. In other words, a central point of the free speech principle is to carry out that commitment.

153

straw man. Really: bulwark against abusive state

There are profound differences between those who emphasize consumer sovereignty and those who stress the democratic roots of the free speech principle. For the latter, government efforts to regulate commercial advertising need not be objectionable. Certainly false and misleading commercial advertising is more readily subject to government control than false and misleading political speech. For those who believe that the free speech principle has democratic foundations and is not fundamentally about consumer sovereignty, government regulation of television, radio, and the Internet need not be objectionable, at least so long as it is reasonably taken as an effort to promote democratic goals.

hot air. crap. Suppose, for example, that government proposes to require television broadcasters (as indeed it now does) to provide three hours per week of educational programming for children. Or suppose that government decides to require television broadcasters to provide a certain amount of free air time for candidates for public office, or a certain amount of time on coverage of elections. For those who believe in consumer sovereignty, these requirements are quite troublesome, indeed they seem like a core violation of the free speech guarantee. For those who associate the free speech principle with democratic goals, these requirements are fully consistent with its highest aspirations. Indeed for many democracies, including for example Germany and Italy, it is well understood that the mass media can be regulated in the interest of improving democratic self-government.[10]

There is nothing novel or iconoclastic in the democratic conception of free speech. On the contrary, this conception lay at the heart of the original understanding of freedom of

does it do the trick?

i.e., mandating regulation?

speech in the United States. In attacking the Alien and Sedition Acts, for example, James Madison claimed that they were inconsistent with the free speech principle, which he linked explicitly to the American transformation of the concept of political sovereignty. In England, Madison noted, sovereignty was vested in the King. But "in the United States, the case is altogether different. The People, not the Government, possess the absolute sovereignty." It was on this foundation that any "Sedition Act" must be judged illegitimate. "[T]he right of electing the members of the Government constitutes . . . the essence of a free and responsible government," and "the value and efficacy of this right depends on the knowledge of the comparative merits and demerits of the candidates for the public trust." It was for this reason that the power represented by a Sedition Act ought, "more than any other, to produce universal alarm; because it is levelled against that right of freely examining public characters and measures, and of free communication among the people thereon, which has ever been justly deemed the only effectual guardian of every other right."[11]

In this way Madison saw "free communication among the people" not as an exercise in consumer sovereignty, in which speech was treated as a kind of commodity, but instead as a central part of self-government, the "only effectual guardian of every other right." Here Madison's conception of free speech was a close cousin of that of Justice Louis Brandeis, who, as we saw in chapter 2, saw public discussion as a "political duty" and believed that the "greatest menace to liberty" would be "an inert people." A central part of the U.S. constitutional tradition, then, places a high premium on speech that

155

is critical to democratic processes, and is hardly hostile to government efforts to promote such speech. If history is our guide, it follows that government efforts to promote a well-functioning system of free expression, as through extensions of the public forum idea, are entirely acceptable. It also follows that government faces special burdens when it attempts to regulate political speech, burdens that are somewhat less ~~more~~ severe than those it faces when it attempts to regulate other forms of speech.

U.S. history is not the only basis for seeing the First Amendment in light of the commitment to democratic deliberation. The argument can be justified by basic principle as well.[12]

Consider, from the democratic point of view, the question whether the free speech principle should be taken to forbid efforts to make communications markets work better. Return to our standard examples: educational programming for children, free air time for candidates for public office, closed-captioning for the hearing-impaired, requirements that Websites contain links to sites with different views. Perhaps some of these proposals would do little or no good, or even harm. But from what standpoint should they be judged inconsistent with the free speech guarantee?

If we believed that the Constitution gives all owners of speech outlets an unbridgeable right to decide what appears on "their" outlets, the answer would be clear: Government could require none of these things. But why should we believe that? We have seen that broadcasters owe their licenses to a government grant, and that owners of Websites enjoy their

proposals for regulation

156

b/cs gov't can turn against the people.
b/cs of fundamental distrust of gov't.

premises w/ no grounding in reality

rights of ownership in large part because of the law, which creates and enforces property rights. None of this means that government can regulate television and the Internet as it chooses. But if government is not favoring any point of view, and if it is really improving the operation of democratic processes, it is hard to find a legitimate basis for complaint. Indeed, the Supreme Court has expressly held that the owners of shopping centers—areas where a great deal of speech occurs—may be required to keep their property open for expressive activity.[13] Shopping centers are not Websites, but if a democratic government is attempting to build on the idea of a public forum, so as to increase the likelihood of exposure to and debate about diverse views, is there really a reasonable objection from the standpoint of free speech itself?

In a similar vein, it makes sense to say that speech that is political in character, in the sense that it relates to democratic self-government, cannot be regulated without an especially strong showing of government justification—and that commercial advertising, obscenity, and other speech that is not political in that sense can be regulated on the basis of a somewhat weaker government justification. I will not attempt to offer a full defense of this idea here, which of course raises some hard line-drawing problems. But in light of the importance of the question to imaginable government regulation of new technologies, there are three points that deserve brief mention.

First, an insistence that government's burden is greatest when it is regulating political speech emerges from a sensible understanding of government's own incentives. It is here that government is most likely to be acting on the basis of illegitimate considerations, such as self-protection, or giving assistance to powerful private groups. Government is least trustworthy when it is attempting to control speech that might harm its own interests; and when speech is political, government's own interests are almost certainly at stake. This is not to deny that government is often untrustworthy when it is regulating commercial speech, art, or other speech that does not relate to democratic self-government. But we have the strongest reasons to distrust government regulation when political issues are involved.

Second, an emphasis on democratic deliberation protects speech not only when regulation is most likely to be biased, but also when regulation is most likely to be harmful. If government regulates sexually explicit speech on the Internet, or requires educational programming for children on television, it remains possible to invoke the normal democratic channels to protest these forms of regulation as ineffectual, intrusive, or worse. But when government forbids criticism of an ongoing war effort, the normal channels are foreclosed, in an important sense, by the very regulation at issue. Controls on public debate are uniquely damaging, because they impair the process of deliberation that is a precondition for political legitimacy.

Third, an emphasis on democratic deliberation is likely to fit, far better than any alternative, with the most reasonable views about particular free speech problems. However much we disagree about the most difficult speech problems, we are likely to believe that at a minimum, the free speech principle protects political expression unless government has exceed-

[handwritten margin note: misses all the sophistication that's actually structuring comm. speech law]

ingly strong grounds for regulating it. On the other hand, forms of speech such as perjury, attempted bribery, threats, unlicensed medical advice, and criminal solicitation are not likely to seem to be at the heart of the free speech guarantee.

An understanding of this kind certainly does not answer all constitutional questions. It does not give a clear test for distinguishing between political and nonpolitical speech, a predictably vexing question.[14] (To those who believe that the absence of a clear test is decisive against the distinction itself, the best response is that any alternative test will lead to line-drawing problems of its own. Because everyone agrees that some forms of speech are regulable, line-drawing is literally inevitable. If you're skeptical, try to think of a test that eliminates problems of this kind.) It does not say whether and when government may regulate art or literature, sexually explicit speech, or libelous speech. In all cases, government is required to have a strong justification for regulating speech, political or not. But the approach I am defending does help to orient inquiry. When government is regulating false or fraudulent commercial advertising, or libel of private persons, or child pornography, it is likely to be on firm ground. When government is attempting to control violent pornography, or speech that contains direct threats of violence aimed at particular people, it need not meet the stringent standards required for regulation of political dissent. All of these points have important implications for the Internet. What I have suggested here, without fully defending the point, is that a conception of the First Amendment that is rooted in democratic deliberation is an exceedingly good place to start.

[handwritten margin note: even here .·.]

FORMS OF NEUTRALITY

None of this means that the government is permitted to regulate the emerging communications market however it wishes. To know whether to object to what government is doing, it is important to know what *kind* of line it is drawing.[15] There are three possibilities here.

1   The government might be regulating speech in a way that is *neutral with respect to the content of the speech at issue*. This is the least objectionable way of regulating speech. For example, government is permitted to say that people may not use loudspeakers on the public streets after midnight or that speakers cannot have access to the front lawn immediately in front of the White House. A regulation of this kind imposes no controls on speech of any particular content. An Internet example: If government says that no one may use CNN's Website unless CNN gives permission, it is acting in a way that is entirely neutral with respect to speech content. So too with restrictions on sending computer viruses. The government bans the ILOVEYOU virus, but it also bans the IHATEYOU virus and the IAMINDIFFERENTTOYOU virus. What is against the law is sending viruses; their content is irrelevant.

2   The government might regulate speech in a way that depends on the content of what is said but without discriminating against any particular point of view. Suppose, for example, that government bans commercial speech on the subways, but allows all other forms of speech on the subways. In the technical language of first amendment law, this form of regulation is "content-based" but "viewpoint-neutral." Consider the old fairness doctrine, which required broadcasters to cover public issues and to allow speech by opposing views. Here the content of speech is highly relevant to what government is requiring; but no specific point of view is punished. In the same category would be a regulation saying that on Websites, sexually explicit speech must be made inaccessible to children. The same can be said for the damages award against the Website of The Nuremburg Trials; the content of the speech definitely mattered, but no particular point of view was being punished. The same award would be given against a Website that treated pro-life people in the same way that The Nuremburg Trials treated doctors. In these cases, no lines are being drawn directly on the basis of point of view.

3 The government might regulate a point of view that it fears or dislikes. This form of regulation is often called "viewpoint discrimination." Government might say, for example, that no one may criticize a decision to go to war, or that no one may claim that one racial group is inferior to another, or that no one may advocate violent overthrow of government.

It makes sense to say that these three kinds of regulations should be treated differently, on new communications media as elsewhere. Viewpoint discrimination is the most objectionable. Content-neutral regulation is the least objectionable. If government is regulating speech because of the point of view that it contains, government's action is almost certainly unconstitutional. Government should not be allowed to censor arguments and positions merely because it disapproves of them. A content-neutral regulation is at the opposite extreme, and most such regulations are entirely legitimate. So long as the basic channels of communications are open, and so long as government has a solid reason for the regulation—for example, to protect people's ability to sleep at night—courts should not intervene if government has regulated in a content-neutral way. Of course a gratuitous or purposeless regulation should be struck down even if it is content-neutral. If government says that the public streets—or for that matter the Internet—may be used for expressive activity, but only between 8:00 P.M. and 8:30 P.M., the neutrality of the regulation is no defense.

Now consider the intermediate case. When government is regulating in a way that is based on content but that is neutral with respect to point of view, there are two issues. The first is whether the particular line being drawn suggests lurking viewpoint discrimination. When it does, the law should probably be struck down. If government says that abortion may not be discussed on television, it is, as a technical matter, discriminating against a topic, but not against any particular point of view; but there is pretty good reason to suspect government's motivations. The second and more fundamental issue is whether government is able to invoke strong, content-neutral grounds for engaging in this form of regulation. A ban on televised discussion of abortion should be struck down for this reason. The ban seems to have no real point, aside from forbidding certain points of view from being expressed.

It doesn't, no matter what you put in it

But the government has a stronger argument if, for example, it is requiring broadcasters to have three hours of educational programming for children. In that case, it is trying to ensure that television serves children, an entirely legitimate interest. And if government is regulating the Internet in an attempt to ensure that people see various sides of public issues, there is good reason to be receptive to what government is trying to do. *containing the risk ??*

Of course some cases may test the line between discrimination on the basis of content and discrimination on the basis of viewpoint. If government is regulating sexually explicit speech when that speech offends contemporary community standards, is it regulating on the basis of viewpoint or merely content? This is not an easy question, and many people have argued over the right answer. But an understanding of the three categories discussed here should be sufficient to make sense out of the bulk of imaginable free speech challenges—and should provide some help in approaching the rest of them as well.

SUBSIDIES AND PENALTIES

Of course government can do a range of things to improve the system of free speech. Here it is important to make one further distinction, between "subsidies" on the one hand and "penalties" on the other. Government is likely to have a great deal of trouble when it is imposing "penalties" on speech. It will have more room to maneuver if it is giving out selective "subsidies." But the distinction between the two is not always obvious.

The most conspicuous "penalties" are criminal and civil punishments. If government makes it a crime to libel people over the Internet or imposes civil fines on television broadcasters who do not provide free airtime for candidates for office, it is punishing speech. The analysis of these penalties should depend on the considerations discussed thus far— whether political speech is involved, what kind of line the government is drawing, and so forth.

Somewhat trickier, but belonging in the same category, are cases in which government is withdrawing a benefit to which people would otherwise be entitled, when the reason for the withdrawal is the government's view about the appropriate content of speech. Suppose, for example, that government gives an annual cash subsidy to all speakers of a certain kind, say those networks that agree to provide educational programming for children. But suppose that government withdraws the subsidy from those networks who provide speech of which the government disapproves—by, say, withdrawing the subsidy from networks whose news shows are critical of the president. For the most part, these sorts of "penalties" should be analyzed in the same way as criminal or civil punishment. When benefits are being withdrawn, as when ordinary punishment is being imposed, government is depriving people of goods to which they would otherwise be entitled, and we may have reason to distrust its motives.

But a quite different issue is posed when government gives out selective subsidies to speakers, as it often does by, for example, funding some museums and artists but not others, and generally through the National Endowment for the Arts and the Public Broadcasting System. Imagine that government is willing to pay for educational programming for children, and pays a station to air that programming on Saturday morning; or that government wants to direct people's attention to certain privately maintained Websites, and hence, pays popular sites, or sites having a certain topic or point of view, to offer an icon for the preferred sites. What is most important here can be stated very simply: *Under current law in the United States (and generally elsewhere), government is permitted to subsidize speech however it wishes.* Government often *is* a speaker, and as such, it is permitted to say whatever it likes. And if government seeks to use taxpayer funds to direct attention to certain sites and topics, there is no basis for constitutional complaint. The only exception to this principle—an exception of unclear content under the law as it now stands—is that if government is allocating funds to private speakers in a way that discriminates on the basis of viewpoint, there might be a First Amendment problem.[16] For example, it would be possible to challenge, on constitutional grounds, a decision by government to fund the Republican Party Website without also funding the Democratic Party Website.

Of course this kind of discrimination goes far beyond anything that I shall be suggesting here. What is important, then, is that government has a great deal of room to maneuver insofar as it is not penalizing speech, but instead subsidizing it.

A RESTRAINED, PRUDENT FIRST AMENDMENT

This chapter has dealt with a range of free speech issues, some of them briskly, and it is important not to lose the forest for the trees. My basic claims have been that the free speech principle is above all a democratic ideal; that it should not be identified with the notion of consumer sovereignty; that it is not an absolute; and that it does not forbid reasonable efforts to promote the goals of republican self-government in the new technological environment. The core requirement of the free speech principle is that with respect to politics, government must remain neutral among points of view. If government is regulating the communications market to promote democratic goals, and if it is not discriminating in favor of or against any point of view, it is acting consistently with the free speech guarantee.

A revised 1A

may gov't prejudice the comm's market gravely, if neutrally? Why does that not violate 1A just the same way a ban on speech on public streets b/twn 8 and 8³⁰ pm would?

policies
and
proposals

There is a large difference between consumers and citizens, and a well-functioning democratic order would be compromised by a fragmented system of communications. Having urged these points, I do not intend to offer a set of detailed policy reforms or any kind of blueprint for the future; this is not a policy manual. But in thinking about reforms, it is important to have some sense of the problems that we aim to address, and of some possible ways of addressing them.

If the discussion thus far is correct, there are three fundamental concerns from the democratic point of view.

1 The need to promote exposure to materials, topics, and positions that people would not have chosen in advance, or at least enough exposure to produce a degree of understanding and curiosity;

2 The value of a range of common experiences; and

3 The need for exposure to substantive questions of policy and principle, combined with a range of positions on such questions.

these disclaimers remind me of those of Larry Summers ('1/'05)

Of course it would be ideal if citizens were demanding, and private providers were creating, a range of initiatives designed to alleviate the underlying concerns. Perhaps they will; promising experiments have been emerging to this effect. Indeed one of my central claims has involved the need for purely private solutions, through a better understanding of what is entailed by the notion of citizenship. New technologies create extraordinary and growing opportunities for exposure to diverse points of view, and indeed growing opportunities for shared experiences and substantive discussions of both policy and principle. It is certainly possible that private choices will lead to far more, not less, in the way of exposure to new topics and viewpoints, and also to more, not less, in the way of shared experiences. But to the extent that they fail to do so, it is worthwhile to consider public initiatives designed to pick up the slack.

Any ideas about how to handle the situation require an understanding of how people are likely to react to topics and points of view that they have not chosen. If, for example, people will never listen to points of view with which they disagree, there would be little point in exposing them to those points of view. If people cannot develop an interest in topics that they would not have chosen, then exposure to those topics is unlikely to be worthwhile. If people would never listen to unchosen views and topics, we might as well build on the emerging capacity of companies to discern and predict tastes, and just allow people to see and hear what they already like. Recall collaborative filtering and Amazon.com's amazing ability to predict what you'll like—simply by combining information about what you've chosen with information about what people who have chosen what you chose have also chosen.

But it seems far more realistic to say that many people—it would be silly to say exactly how many, but surely millions—are prepared to listen to points of view that they have not selected. Many people are also prepared to develop an interest in topics that they would not choose and in fact know nothing about. To work well, a deliberative democracy had better have many such people. It cannot function without them. And if many people are able to benefit from wider exposure, it is worthwhile to think about ways to improve the communications market to their, and our, advantage.

that so?

I briefly discuss six reform possibilities here:

1 deliberative domains; *we have*

2 disclosure of relevant conduct by producers of communications;

3 voluntary self-regulation;

4 economic subsidies, including publicly subsidized programming and Websites;

to what?

5 "must-carry" rules, in the form of links, imposed on the most popular Websites, designed to produce exposure to substantive questions; and

6 "must-carry" rules, also in the form of links, imposed on highly partisan Websites, designed to ensure that viewers learn about sites with opposing views, perhaps through linked sites and perhaps through hyperlinks.

Of course different proposals would work better, or differently, for some communications outlets than for others, and I will draw attention to some of these differences here.

even if run by private individuals.

Disclosure of public affairs programming, for example, is more sensibly required for television and radio broadcasters than for Websites. Almost all of the proposals could be implemented through private action (the preferred approach by far), public regulation (the least preferred approach, though sometimes necessary), or through creative combinations of the two.

DELIBERATIVE DOMAINS

It would be extremely valuable to have several widely publicized deliberative domains on the Internet, ensuring opportunities for discussion among people with diverse views. In chapter 3, we encountered James Fishkin's deliberative opinion poll, attempting to describe public opinion not after telephone calls to people in their homes for unreflective responses, but as a result of extended discussions in groups of heterogeneous people. Along with several others, Fishkin is now engaged in a process of creating deliberative opportunities on the Internet—spaces where people with different views can meet and exchange reasons, and have a chance to understand, at least a bit, the point of view of those who disagree with them. The hope is that citizen engagement, mutual understanding, and better thinking will emerge as a result.

Imagine, for example, a new Website: deliberativedemocracy.com—or if you wish, deliberativedemocracy.org. (Neither name is currently taken; I've checked.) The site could easily be created by the private sector. When you come to the site, you might find a general description of goals and contents. Everyone would understand that this is a place where people of very different views are invited to listen and to speak. And once you're there, you would be able to read and (if you wish) participate in discussions of a topic of your choice, by clicking on icons involving, for example, civil rights, the environment, unemployment, foreign affairs, the stock market, children, gun control, labor unions, and much more. Many of these topics might have icons with smaller subtopics—under environment, for example, there might be discussions of global warming, genetically engineered food, water pollution, and hazardous waste sites. Each topic and subtopic could provide brief descriptions of agreed-upon facts and competing points of view, as an introduction and frame for the discussion. Private creativity, on the part of users, would undoubtedly take things in boundless unanticipated directions. Private managers of such sites would have their own norms about how people should interact with one another; deliberativedemocracy.com, for example, might encourage norms of civility. *bloggers ?*

Many such experiments are now emerging, sometimes self-consciously, sometimes through the kinds of spontaneous developments that occur on e-mail and listserves. For obvious reasons, there would be many advantages to a situation in which a few such sites were especially prominent. If this were the case, deliberativedemocracy.com, for example, would have a special salience for many citizens, providing a forum in which hundreds of thousands, or even millions, could participate, if only through occasional reading. But we should hardly be alarmed if a large number of deliberative Websites were to emerge and to compete with one another. Perhaps government could provide a funding mechanism to subsidize the development of some such sites without having a managerial role (see below). But what is most important is general awareness of the importance of deliberation to a well-functioning democracy, and of deliberation among people who do not agree. If that awareness is widespread, sites of the sort that I am describing here will grow up entirely on their own.

DISCLOSURE: SUNLIGHT AS DISINFECTANT

The last decades have seen an extraordinary growth in the use of a simple regulatory tool: require people to disclose what they are doing. In the environmental area, this has been an exceptionally effective strategy. Probably the most striking example is the Emergency Planning and Community Right-to-Know Act (EPCRA). Under this statute, firms and individuals must report to state and local government the quantities of potentially hazardous chemicals that have been stored or released into the environment. This has been an amazing and unanticipated success story: Mere disclosure, or threat of disclosure, has resulted in voluntary, low-cost reductions in toxic releases. It is no wonder that disclosure has become a popular approach to dealing with pollution. When polluters are required to disclose their actions, political pressures or market pressures will lead to reductions without any need for actual government mandates.

A great deal of recent attention has also been given to disclosure requirements in the communications industry. Suppose, for example, that certain programming might be harmful to children, and that certain other programming might be beneficial to society. Is there a way for government to discourage the bad and to encourage the good, without regulating speech directly? Disclosure requirements suggest a minimally intrusive possibility. Thus the mandatory "v-chip" is intended to permit parents to block programming that they want to exclude from their homes; the v-chip is supposed to work hand-in-hand with a ratings system giving information about the suitability of programming for children of various ages. Similarly, a provision of the 1996 Telecommunications Act imposes three relevant requirements. Television manufacturers must include technology capable of reading a program rating mechanism; the FCC must create a ratings methodology if the industry does not produce an acceptable ratings plan within a year; and broadcasters must include a rating in their signals if the relevant program is rated. The ratings system has now been in place for several years, and it seems to have been, at the very worst, a partial success, making it far simpler and easier for parents to monitor what children are seeing.

A chief advantage of the disclosure strategy is its comparative flexibility. If viewers know the content of television programs in advance, they can use market pressures, by refusing to watch; broadcasters are of course responsive to widespread refusals. People can also impose more political pressures by complaining to stations or to elected representatives, and here too it is possible to induce changes. From the democratic point of view, regulation via disclosure also has substantial virtues. A well-functioning system of deliberative democracy requires a certain degree of information so that citizens can engage in their monitoring and deliberative tasks. A good way to enable citizens to oversee private or public action, and also to assess the need for less, more, or different regulation, is to inform them of both private and public activity. The very fact that the public will be in a position to engage in general monitoring may well be a spur to desirable outcomes.

Disclosure could be used in many different ways, suitable for different communications media. Disclosure requirements of various sorts might, for example, be imposed on television broadcasters, radio broadcasters, cable television, and Website providers. The idea here, associated with Justice Louis Brandeis, is that "sunlight is the best of disinfectants."

It is obviously easier to impose disclosure requirements on radio and television broadcasters, relatively few in number and publicly licensed in any case, than on Websites. The idea would be to ensure that anyone who is engaging in a practice that might produce harm, or do less good than might be done, should be required to disclose that fact to the public.[1] The disclosure might or might not alter behavior. If it does not alter behavior, we have reason to believe that the public is not much concerned about it. If the behavior does change, the public was, in all likelihood, sufficiently exercised to demand it.

As an illustration, consider a simple proposal: _Broadcasters should be required to disclose, in some detail and on a quarterly basis, all of their public service and public interest activities._ The disclosure might include an accounting of any free airtime provided to candidates, opportunities to speak for those addressing public issues, rights of reply, educational programming, charitable activities, programming designed for traditionally underserved communities, closed captioning for the hearing impaired, local programming, and public service announcements. Astonishingly, radio and television broadcasters have yet to disclose this information to the public, though initial information gathering has been done by the NAB. A hope, vindicated by similar approaches in environmental law, is that a disclosure requirement will by itself trigger improved performance, by creating a kind of competition to do more and better, and by enlisting various social pressures in the direction of improved performance.

I have referred several times to the old fairness doctrine, which required broadcasters to cover public issues and to allow a right of reply for dissenting views. We have seen that this doctrine was largely repealed, on the ground that it chilled coverage of public issues in the first instance. We have also seen that insofar as the repeal has increased fragmentation and hence polarization, it has produced genuine problems. But even for those who approve of the old fairness doctrine, a disclosure requirement could be far less intrusive way of accomplishing the same basic goals. It is quite possible that such a requirement would produce some movement toward more coverage of public issues and more attention to diverse views. It is even possible that such a requirement would help to address the three problems identified at the beginning of this chapter.

It is also possible that any disclosure requirement would produce no movement at all. But notice that people did not anticipate that the Toxic Release Inventory would by itself spur reductions in toxic releases, as it emphatically did. For voluntary improvements to occur, the disclosure requirements must be accompanied by economic or political pressure of some kind, perhaps from external monitors, or at least a degree of conscience on the part of producers. If there are external monitors, and if those monitors are able to impose reputational or financial costs on those with bad records, disclosure is likely to do some good.

The external monitors might include public interest groups seeking to shame badly performing broadcasters; they might include rivals who seek to create a kind of "race to the top," in the form of better performance; they might include newspaper reporters and Websites. Consider radio and television broadcasting. If public interest organizations, and viewers who favor certain programming, are able to mobilize, perhaps in concert with certain members of the mass media, substantial improvements might be expected. It is even possible that a disclosure requirement would help create its own monitors. And in view of the relative unintrusiveness of a disclosure requirement, and the flexibility of any private responses, this approach is certainly worth trying. At worst, little will be lost. At most, something will be gained, probably in the form of better programming and greater information about the actual performance of the industry. In light of the aspirations of most viewers, the possible result of disclosure will be to improve the quality and quantity of both educational and civic programming in a way that promotes the goals of a well-functioning deliberative democracy.

My emphasis here has been on the application of disclosure requirements to television and radio broadcasters. But in one or another form, such requirements might be imposed on other information providers, such as cable television and Websites. The current ratings requirements, involving suitability for children, apply to cable programs as well as to broadcasters. Websites already inform people of content unsuitable for children. It would be easy to build on these ideas, so that people would be aware that they have arrived at a site with sexually explicit material, and so that they can "block" such sites if they choose. Other disclosure requirements could undoubtedly help both consumers and citizens.

VOLUNTARY SELF-REGULATION

A somewhat more aggressive approach, going beyond disclosure, would be to encourage voluntary self-regulation by those who provide information. One of the most noteworthy trends of the last two decades, inside and outside the world of communications, has been in the direction of self-regulation designed to protect social goals.[2] Websites might, for example, be encouraged to agree, among each other but without government mandates, to provide privacy guarantees to those who "visit." Radio stations might agree, perhaps via some kind of Code of Conduct, to attempt to provide a wide range of views on public issues, so as to ensure that listeners encounter something other than a loud version of what they already think.

One of the motivating ideas behind voluntary self-regulation is that competition among producers can be harmful from the point of view of the public as a whole. Endless efforts to get people's attention may do long-term damage. Everyone knows that there has been an increasing trend toward "tabloidization," with mainstream newspapers emphasizing scandals and sensationalism. This trend predated the Internet, but it has been accelerated by its existence. Often the news seems not to involve news at all; sometimes it seems to

177

) contest that

no! It's a broadcast phenomenon, nullified by the rise of bloggers and partisan cable shows

be a continuation of the fictional drama that preceded it, with detailed discussion of the "real life events" mirrored in the fiction. Many journalists worry about this problem. As Robert Frank and Philip Cook warn, with reference to the effects of market forces,

> Increasingly impoverished political debate is yet another cost of our current cultural trajectory. Complex modern societies generate complex economic and social problems, and the task of choosing the best course is difficult under the best of circumstances. And yet, as in-depth analysis and commentary give way to sound bites in which rival journalists and politicians mercilessly ravage one another, we become an increasingly ill-informed and ill-tempered electorate.[3]

An agreement among producers can break (or brake) this competition and hence perform some of the valuable functions of law—but without intruding law into the domain of speech regulation.

With respect to television, consider the possibility of promoting democratic goals through voluntary self-regulation, as through a Code of Conduct to be issued and enforced by the NAB or perhaps by a wider range of those who produce television for the American public. For many decades, in fact, the NAB did administer such a code, partly to promote its economic interests (by raising the price of advertising), partly to fend off regulation (by showing that the industry was engaged in beneficial self-regulation, making government efforts unnecessary), and partly to carry out the moral commitments of broadcasters themselves. Notably, voluntary self-regulation has played a role in numerous areas of media policy, including, for example, cigarette advertising, children's advertising, family viewing, advertising of hard liquor, and fairness in news reporting. In the 1980s, continuing congressional concern about televised violence led to a new law creating an antitrust exemption for networks, broadcasters, cable operators and programmers, and trade associations, precisely to permit them to generate standards to reduce the amount of violence on television. As we have seen, a ratings system for television is now in place, and it should be treated as a successful example of voluntary self-regulation, giving parents a general sense of the appropriateness of programming

A new code might address a number of the problems discussed thus far. For example, signatories could agree to cover substantive issues in a serious way, to avoid sensationalistic treatment of politics, to give extended coverage to public issues, and to allow diverse voices to be heard. In fact ideas of this kind long played a role in the television industry until the abandonment of the broadcasters' code in 1979. In view of the increasing range of options, and the declining centrality of television broadcasters, there are undoubtedly limits to how much can be done through this route. But in many contexts, voluntary self-regulation of this kind has produced considerable good, and codes of some kind could provide a sort of quality assurance to the public. We might easily imagine, for example, agreements among broadcasters and cable television dealing with programming for children, emergency situations, and perhaps coverage of elections. It is also possible to imagine agreements among Websites, designed to protect children, to ensure privacy, and to promote attention to

179

diverse views. If market forces are producing serious problems, we have every reason to encourage creative thinking in this vein.

SUBSIDIES

A third possibility, also with an established history, would involve government subsidies. With respect to television and radio, many nations, including the United States, have relied on a combination of private and public funding. In the United States, the Public Broadcasting System (PBS) is designed to provide programming that, it is believed, will find insufficient funding in the private domain, including educational programming for children. Interestingly, and contrary to common belief, most of PBS's funding comes from private sources; the government provides a subsidy in the form of about 17 percent of PBS's budget. This is a genuine public-private partnership.

The traditional rationale for a separate public broadcasting station has been weakened by the proliferation of options, including many, on both television and the Internet, that provide discussion of public issues and education for children. This is not to say that the rationale has been eliminated. About one-third of Americans continue to rely on over-the-air broadcasting, and many of them benefit from, and depend on, PBS. Nor do I mean to suggest that in all respects, the situation is better now than it was when the universe of options was so much smaller. In a system with four stations, PBS had a kind of salience that it now lacks, and it is by no means clear that the current situation, with dozens or hundreds of avail-

with Paul Wolfowitz in charge, or Robert Reich?

able stations, is in all respects an improvement for all children or all adults. But with many private outlets doing the same kind of thing, it does seem clear that the rationale for PBS, in its current form, gets a bit weaker every day.

What, if anything, might be done instead? Internet specialist Andrew Shapiro, concerned about many of the problems identified here, offers an intriguing suggestion.[4] Shapiro says that the government should support a special Website, Public.Net, dedicated to discussion of issues of the day from many different points of view. Public.Net would provide an icon, visible on your home computer. You would be under no obligation to click on it; indeed, its visibility may even be an annoyance to you, and in a free society perhaps you should be permitted to remove the icon if you really do not like it. But if the proposal works well, at least a significant number of people—not a majority, but enough—would be sufficiently intrigued to see, on occasion, what is being discussed there. And if many people are interested, then the program is likely to be worthwhile and would pick up speed and momentum. Perhaps Public.Net would have sections like those described above for deliberativedemocracy.com— environment, civil rights, gun control, foreign affairs, and so forth. Doubtless private and public creativity would move Public.Net in many unanticipated directions.

Of course there are dangers in any system in which government manages and controls a public Website. Probably the best approach would be to ensure, not government management and control, but a mixture of government and commercial subsidies to a non-profit, non-governmental space. Indeed, we could easily imagine a range of such spaces, designed

181

to ensure a range of arenas for public deliberation on the Internet. As we have seen, modest private experiments in this direction are emerging; we should hope for much more in this vein. The PBS model should be updated. It is past time to consider new initiatives that make better sense in the new communications environment.

"MUST CARRY": CONSTITUTIONAL DEBATES

Some of the most interesting developments in the law of speech involve "access rights" or "must carry" rules. In fact the public forum doctrine creates a kind of "must carry" rule for streets and parks. These sites must be opened up for speech. You and I are entitled to have access to them. Is there any place for "must carry" rules on the Internet, or in the current technological environment? Could Congress say that Web-sites must carry certain links? *Absolutely not!*

To answer these questions, and as preface for discussion of policy options, it is necessary to have some sense of the legal background. In the 1970s, the Supreme Court held that government has the authority to subject television and radio broadcasters to a kind of "must carry" rule, in the form of the old fairness doctrine, requiring attention to public issues and an opportunity for diverse views to speak.[5] At the same time, the Court rejected the idea that private newspapers may be treated as public forums and subject to "must carry" rules.[6] The apparent difference between broadcasters and news-papers—fragile in the 1970s, and still more fragile today—is that the former are "scarce," largely for technological reasons, and hence are more properly subject to governmental controls.

could Congress outlaw TiVo on the same grounds?

Now that the scarcity rationale has weakened, the continued viability of the fairness doctrine remains an open question. If the FCC tried to reinstate the doctrine, the Court might strike it down. But the Court has nonetheless upheld legislation that imposes "must carry" rules on cable television providers.[7] The relevant legislation, still on the books, requires cable providers to set aside a number of their channels for both "local commercial television stations" and "noncommercial educational television stations." Congress defended these requirements as a way of ensuring the economic viability of broadcasters, on whom many millions of Americans continue to rely (about 30% as of 2000). In finding the "must carry" requirements constitutional, the Court said, "assuring that the public has access to a multiplicity of information sources is a governmental purpose of the highest order, for it promotes values central to the First Amendment." The Court also emphasized the "potential for abuse of . . . private power over a central avenue of communication," and stressed that the Constitution "does not disable the government from taking steps to ensure that private interests not restrict, through physical control of a critical pathway of communication, the free flow of information and ideas."[8]

In so saying, the Court was recalling Justice Brandeis' emphatically republican conception of the First Amendment. Indeed, Justice Breyer, in a separate opinion, made the link with Justice Brandeis explicit: The statute's "policy, in turn, seeks to facilitate the public discussion and informed deliberation, which, as Justice Brandeis pointed out many years ago, democratic government presupposes and the First Amendment seeks to achieve."[9] Here, then, is an unambiguous

since that's a universal condition, it is of no analytic interest

endorsement of the idea that government has the power to regulate communications technologies to promote goals associated with deliberative democracy.

So far, so good. But for those interested in thinking about the implications of the Court's decision for the Internet and other technologies, there is considerable ambiguity in the case. How crucial was it, to the Court's reasoning, that the cable provider controlled access to cable stations? Suppose that a speaker seeks a right of access to a particular Website, and complains that he is excluded by private power (made possible of course by law). Might "private power" also be a problem if, as with the Internet, there are countless other available Websites, and indeed if speakers seeking access to one particular Website are permitted to create Websites of their own? The Court does not say. The constitutional status of other sorts of "must carry" rules, and other rights of access, is unclear.

LINKS, HYPERLINKS, AND THE SCARCE COMMODITY OF ATTENTION

A central issue for the future will involve the use of links and hyperlinks, designed to heighten or to decrease the risk of fragmentation. To understand that issue, return to the fact that one of the most important of all commodities, in the current situation, is people's attention. This is what companies are endlessly competing to obtain. Much activity on the Internet, by those interested in profits and other goods, is designed to produce greater attention, even if only for a moment. If a company or a political candidate can get attention from ten thousand people for as little as two seconds, it will have accomplished a great deal.

Almost everyone has noticed that many Websites do not, and need not, charge a fee for users. If you want to go to WashingtonPost.com, or NewYorkTimes.com, or NewRepublic.com, you can do so for free, and hence you can get the content of countless magazines and newspapers without paying a penny. Nor is the phenomenon limited to magazines and newspapers. If you want to learn about cancer, for example, you can find out a great deal from oncology.com, entirely free of charge. Why is this? It is because advertisers are willing to foot the bill. What advertisers are buying is access, and usually brief access at that, to people's eyes—a small period of attention.

Here again we can see that those who use Websites are commodities at least as much as they are consumers; they are what Websites are selling to advertisers for a fee, sometimes a large one. Targeting and customization are playing a large role here, as advertisers come to learn, with some precision, how many people, and which people, visit from which advertisements. Of course advertisements cannot guarantee sales. Most people who see an icon for Bloomingdale's or Amazon. com will simply ignore it. But some will not; they will be curious and see what there is to see. Or they will file it away in some part of their minds for future use.

If we combine an understanding of access rights and "must carry" rules with an appreciation of the crucial role of attention, we might enlist advertisers' practices in the service of public interest goals. In other words, people in the private and public sector, knowing that attention is valuable, might

on prime real estate? Above the fold? Or on p. 217?

think of ways to capture that attention, not to coerce people, but to trigger their interest in material that might produce individual and social benefits. Links among sites are the obvious strategy here. Ideally, such links would be provided voluntarily. It might also be worthwhile to consider legislation designed to ensure more in the way of links and hyperlinks, on a viewpoint-neutral basis.

LINKED SITES

In the context of the Internet, the point of "carrying," or "must carry," is to get people's attention, however fleetingly. Consider in this light a proposal: Providers of material with a certain point of view might also provide access to sites with a very different point of view. Townhall.com, a site featuring conservative opinions, might agree to provide icons for liberal sites, in return for an agreement, from those sites, to provide icons for sites carried on Townhall.com. The icon itself would not require anyone to read anything. It would merely provide a signal, to the viewer, that there is a place where a different point of view might be consulted. Of the thousands or millions of people who choose any particular site, not most, but undoubtedly a few, would be sufficiently interested to look further. Best of all, this form of "carriage" would replicate many features of the public street and the general interest intermediary. It would alert people to the existence of materials other than those they read. We have seen that some sites do this already. The problem is that the practice remains unusual.

We could even imagine a situation in which many partisan sites offer a links page saying something like, "We have a clear point of view, and we hope that more people will come to believe what we do. But we are also committed to democratic debate and to discussion among people who think differently. To that end we are providing links to other sites, in the interest of providing genuine debate on these issues." If many sites would agree to do this, the problem of fragmentation might be substantially reduced.

There is another possibility. Especially popular Websites could provide links to a random draw of sites designed to educate people and to promote attention to public issues.[10] The random draw of links might change every month, or every week, or even every day. All that would be required would be the display of an icon. It would be up to you to decide whether to visit the site. We could easily imagine a situation in which (say) the twenty-five most popular sites, in any two-month period, provided icons for a random draw of many other sites dealing with public questions. Of course this is only a sketch; the details could be filled in various different ways.

HYPERLINKS

For those who object to intrusions on the siteowner's control over the site itself, other approaches might be imagined. The simplest would be to increase the use of hyperlinks. Consider the fact that when you use LEXIS, the legal research tool, and call up any judicial opinion, you will see, in that opinion, references to other judicial opinions and occasionally

but readers already have instant access. This entire argument is silly because it's futile and unnecessary.

academic writing; those references are hyperlinks, enabling you to click on them and thus to get immediate access to the document in question. Many sites now offer a similar feature. In some cases, for example, a book title given in a review or discussion will operate as a hyperlink; if you click on it, you will immediately go to a site from which you can purchase the book in question.

We might easily imagine a situation in which textual references to organizations or institutions are hyperlinks, so that if, for example, a conservative magazine such as the *National Review* refers to the World Wildlife Fund or Environmental Defense, it also allows readers instant access to their sites. As compared with links in the form of advertisements, the advantage of the hyperlink approach is that it is less costly to the siteowner and less intrusive on its prerogatives—indeed, it is barely an intrusion at all. The disadvantage is that a hyperlink is generally less attention-grabbing than an advertisement. Here as elsewhere, the ideal would be for sites to do this on their own, not through government mandates. In chapter 3 we saw that it is common for political sites to offer links to like-minded sites, but quite uncommon for them to offer links to those with opposed views. We could easily imagine the emergence of a new and good democratic custom: Sites would generally ensure that references to other organizations are hyperlinks too.

To the extent that sites do not do this, voluntary self-regulation through cooperative agreements might do the job. If these routes do not work, it would be worthwhile considering content-neutral regulation, designed to ensure more in the way of both links and hyperlinks. To be sure, free speech

Google does all that already.
You're stuck in an outmoded technological paradigm

problems could be raised here—especially in light of the danger that a requirement of hyperlinks might discourage references to opposing groups in the first instance. What is most important is that we could easily imagine a situation in which links or hyperlinks were the ordinary practice, used in a way that would promote goals of both consumers and citizens, without compromising the legitimate interest of site owners.

Weak?

There are other possible approaches, more and less radical. For example, those who choose to visit certain sites—say, especially popular ones or ones with distinctive political views—might automatically be connected, at certain times, to sites maintained by those seeking access. Drawing on the public forum analogy, law and technology specialist Noah Zatz has suggested that through this route, "sidewalks" might be created in cyberspace, allowing speakers to have "specific access" to certain users, subject to reasonable time, place, and manner restrictions.[11] An obvious objection is that many people would find this intrusive. Attempting to have access to the Website of *Time* magazine, they might find themselves opening a page to Citizens for Control of Nuclear Power as well. This is indeed an intrusion. But is it much different from daily life on a street or in a park? Is it much different from reading the newspaper or a general interest magazine? Because it is so easy to close a Webpage, any intrusion on Internet users seems far more trivial than those introduced via public forums and general interest intermediaries, intrusions that produce many benefits. What is important about Zatz's proposal is not the relatively complex details, which I do not mean to endorse, but the effort to adapt technology to the service of goals associated with the public forum doctrine.

by the government

• What's troubling here is the extreme technological shallowness of the argument.

189

THE TYRANNY OF THE STATUS QUO *is dead*

The tyranny of the status quo has many sources. Sometimes it is based on a fear of unintended consequences, as in the economists' plea, "the perfect is the enemy of the good"— a mantra of resignation to which we should respond, with John Dewey, that "the better is the enemy of the still better." Sometimes it is grounded in a belief, widespread though palpably false, that things cannot be different from what they now are. Sometimes reforms seem to be hopelessly utopian, far too much so to be realistic. And sometimes they seem small and incremental, even silly, and to do nothing large enough to solve the underlying problems.

The suggestions I have offered here are modest and incremental. They are designed to give some glimpses of the possibilities and also to do at least a little bit of good. Some of them are now under active discussion. What is especially important, in the current era, is that we retain a sense of the grounds on which we can evaluate them. To those skeptical of the proposals outlined here, on the ground that they are too intrusive or too tepid, it makes sense to ask: If we seek to enlist current technologies in the service of democratic ideals, what reforms would be better? —— *hands off. Let creativity flourish!*

or too futile

Deregulate / P as much as possible.

conclusion:
republic.com

Much of what I have argued here is captured in some passages from two great theorists of freedom and democracy, John Stuart Mill and John Dewey. First Mill:

> It is hardly possible to overstate the value, in the present state of human improvement, of placing human beings in contact with other persons dissimilar to themselves, and with modes of thought and action unlike those with which they are familiar. . . . Such communication has always been, and is peculiarly in the present age, one of the primary sources of progress.[1]

And now Dewey:

> The belief that thought and its communication are now free simply because legal restrictions which once obtained have been done away is absurd. Its currency perpetuates the infantile state of social knowledge. For it blurs recognition of our central need to possess conceptions which are used as tools of directed inquiry and which are tested, rectified and caused to grow in actual

191

Google searches will often bring up the contrary, thus acting like a sidewalk

use. No man and no mind was ever emancipated merely by being left alone? *And that's where the Internet is so helpful.*

With these ideas in view, I have stressed the severe problems, for individuals and societies alike, that are likely to be created by the practice of self-insulation—by a situation in which many of us wall ourselves off from the concerns and opinions of our fellow citizens. The ideal of consumer sovereignty, well-represented in the supposedly utopian vision of complete "personalization," could produce severe risks for a democracy. Rather than a utopian vision, it is best understood *Same* as a kind of nightmare, the stuff of science fiction, carrying large lessons about some neglected requirements of democratic self-government.

a totally unrealistic fear; a true red herring

more so than we have?

WITHIN AND WITHOUT ENCLAVES

A market dominated by countless versions of the "Daily Me" would make self-government less workable. In many ways it would reduce, not increase, freedom for the individuals involved. It would create a high degree of social fragmentation. It would make mutual understanding far more difficult among individuals and groups. Of course many people will be sufficiently curious to use new technologies to see a wide range of topics and views. Millions are now doing exactly that. But fragmentation, and group polarization, are significant risks even if only a relatively small proportion of people chooses to listen and speak with those who are like minded. A free society creates public domains containing a wide variety of people and positions.

192

groups with strongly developed views, traditions, rules, etc., can be created/maintained only with a fair amount of chosen orthodoxy. Why is child raising such an issue today?

strongly contest this claim. Also, we need

Nothing in these claims is inconsistent with the view that a free society also makes spaces for deliberating enclaves, consisting of like-minded individuals. As we have seen, such enclaves ensure that positions that would otherwise be silenced or squelched have a chance to develop. Individual members of such groups sometimes have a hard time communicating their views to the wider society, and the ability of such individuals to speak among themselves can be an individual and social good.

Although I have suggested that group polarization and local cascades present serious dangers, similar phenomena played an unquestionable role in movements that have and deserve widespread approval: To take just a few examples, consider the attack on apartheid in South Africa, the civil rights movement in the United States, the assault on slavery itself. Nor are group polarization and local cascades merely a matter of historical interest. Consider, for example, private conversations among African-Americans, political dissenters, poor tenants, and members of religious minorities. Insofar as new technologies make it easier to construct enclaves for communication among people with common experiences and complaints, they are a boon as well as a danger. Internet discussion groups, for example, can allow people to discuss shared difficulties when they would otherwise feel quite isolated and believe that their condition is unique or in any case hopeless. This is highly desirable for the people involved and also for society as a whole.

The danger of such enclaves should by now be familiar. Their members may move to positions that lack merit but are predictable consequences of the particular pressures produced

193

Because everyone listens to experts, has no traditions to fall back upon, is deracinated. Deracination is a far bigger problem for democracy than isolation.

So why not force, say, orthodox Jews to throw open their closed communities?

by deliberation among the like-minded. In the extreme case, enclave deliberation may even put social stability at risk (sometimes for better, usually for worse). What I have suggested is that it would be extremely unfortunate if new technologies were used so as to increase the likelihood that members of deliberating enclaves will wall themselves off from opposing views.

But it is not difficult to imagine a very different kind of vision, one directly opposed to that offered by the "Daily Me." Suppose, for example, that most people generally believed it important to seek out diverse opinions and to learn about an assortment of topics. Suppose, in other words, that the extraordinary opportunities provided by the Internet and other technological developments were regularly used as an instrument of citizenship, mostly national but sometimes even global, in which people continually enlarged their own horizons, often testing their own views by learning about alternatives. We could easily imagine a general social norm to this effect, even a cultural shift, toward a society in which people were generally committed to using new technologies in this way.

We could also imagine a culture where aspirations of this kind were supported rather than undermined by private and public institutions. In such a culture, Websites would frequently assist people in their desire to learn about other opinions, even opinions different from those of the Websites' creators. In such a culture, it would be common to provide links to sites with a wide range of views. And in such a culture, government would attempt, through unintrusive measures to

why does that follow? On the contrary, speech is far too valuable to let gov't mwe co/it

the extent possible, to ensure that the system of communications was a help rather than a hindrance to democratic self-government.

CONSUMER AND CITIZEN

Many people think that a system of communications should be evaluated by asking whether it respects individual choice. In this view, the only real threat to free speech is "censorship," conventionally understood. Speech is simply another commodity, to be chosen by consumers subject to the forces of supply and demand. With respect to ordinary consumer products, it seems natural to believe that the more people can "customize," or individuate, their preferred products, the better things will be. A well-functioning market for toasters, cars, chocolates, and computers seems to work better if it allows a large domain for individual choice— so that I will not have the same item that you have, unless this is what we want, in our individual capacities.

We have seen, however, that insofar as the Internet increases consumer choice, it is not an unmixed blessing for consumers. The "consumption treadmill" means that for many products, people's purchases of more and better goods will make them spend more, and possibly much more, without really making them happier or improving their lives. But the more fundamental problem is that a system of free expression should not be seen in terms of consumers and consumption at all. In a free republic, such a system is designed to maintain the conditions for democratic self-government—to serve citizens,

who does the serving?

not consumers. Hence the public forum doctrine ensures that the streets and parks are open to speakers, even if many of us, much of the time and before the fact, would prefer not to hear what our fellow citizens want to say.

When the public forum doctrine was originally devised, in the early twentieth century, avoiding streets and parks was far more difficult than it is today; hence the public forum doctrine had immense practical importance. But this is decreasingly true. It is now entirely possible, and indeed increasingly possible, to spend little time in public forums. Largely by happenstance, general interest intermediaries of the middle and late twentieth century—those who operate newspapers, magazines, and broadcasting stations—have done much of the historical work of traditional streets and parks. They promote exposure to issues and views that would otherwise escape attention, and that would not have been chosen before the fact. At the same time, they ensure a commonality of experience in a heterogeneous society.

In a free society, those who want to avoid general interest intermediaries are certainly permitted to do so. No government agency compels adults to read or to watch. Nonetheless, a central democratic goal is to ensure a large measure of social integration—not merely of racial groups, but across multiple lines, in a way that broadens sympathies and enriches human life. A society with general interest intermediaries, like a society with a robust set of public forums, promotes a shared set of experiences at the same time that it exposes countless people to information and opinions that they would not have sought out in advance. These features of a well-functioning system of free expression might well be compromised when individuals can personalize their own communications packages.

I have emphasized throughout that a republic is not a direct democracy, and that a good democratic system contains institutions designed to ensure a measure of reflection and debate—not immediate responses to whatever people at any particular moment in time, happen to say that they want. In this way, the original U.S. Constitution was based on a commitment to a set of "filters" of a special kind—filters that would increase the likelihood of deliberation in government. The same commitment can be found in most democratic nations, which ensure against reflexive responses to popular pressures. Insofar as new technologies make it easier for people to register their short-term views, and induce government to respond, they carry risks rather than promise. But insofar as new technologies make it easier for people to deliberate with one another, and to exchange reasons, they might carry forward some of the animating ideals of the system of free expression.

We have seen as well that it is unhelpful and implausible to say that with respect to the Internet, and other communications technologies, "no regulation" is the path for the future. Any system that protects property rights requires an active governmental role, and that role takes the form of regulation, among other things allowing "owners," owing their status as such to law, to exclude people seeking access. If site owners and operators are going to be protected against "cyber-terrorism" and other intrusions on their property rights, government and law (not to mention taxpayers) will play a central role. The question is not whether we shall have regulation, but what kind of regulation we shall have. *come on!*

the universalizing arg + again

197

doesn't support premise

Free speech is never an absolute. Every democratic system regulates some forms of speech, not merely by creating property rights, but also by controlling a variety of forms of expression, such as perjury, bribery, threats, child pornography, and fraudulent commercial advertising (not to mention viruses sent by e-mail). The question is not whether we will regulate speech, but how—and in particular how we can do so while promoting the values associated with a system of free expression, emphatically including democratic self-government.

I have also stressed the relationship between freedom of expression and many important social goals. When information is freely available, tyrannies are unlikely to be able to sustain themselves; it is for this reason that the Internet is a great engine of democratic self-government. Drawing on the work of economist Amartya Sen, and with particular reference to new technologies, I have also suggested that freedom of expression is central to social well-being, precisely because of the pressures that it places on governments. Recall Sen's finding that no society with a free press and open elections has ever experienced a famine. We should take this finding as a metaphor for the functions of freedom of expression in ensuring that governments serve the interest of their people, rather than the other way around.

BEYOND PESSIMISM, NOSTALGIA, AND PREDICTION

I have made three more particular suggestions. First, a communications system granting individuals an unlimited power to filter threatens to create excessive fragmentation. It would do this if different individuals and groups, defined in demographic, religious, political, or other terms, choose materials and viewpoints that fit with their own predilections, while excluding topics and viewpoints that do not. This would undoubtedly produce a more balkanized society. The danger is greatly heightened by the phenomenon of group polarization, through which deliberating groups move toward a more extreme point in the same direction indicated by their pre-deliberation judgments. Indeed, the Internet creates a large risk of group polarization, simply because it makes it so easy for like-minded people to speak with one another—and ultimately to move toward extreme and sometimes even violent positions. All too often, those most in need of hearing something other than echoes of their own voices are least likely to seek out alternative views. Often the result can be cybercascades of a highly undesirable sort, as false information spreads to thousands or even millions. We have seen evidence to this effect most vividly for extremist and racist organizations, but the point is far more general than that.

Second, a system of unlimited filtering could produce too little in the way of shared information and experiences. When many or most people are focusing on the same topic, at least some of the time, a system of freedom creates a kind of social glue. The point is all the more important in light of the fact that information is a public good—a good whose benefits are likely to spread well beyond the particular person who receives it. General interest intermediaries provide many advantages in this regard, simply because most of us obtain information that we then spread to others, and from which they benefit.

Third, a system of unlimited filtering might well compromise freedom, understood from the democratic point of view.

i.e. gov't   *in other words, The State*

For citizens in a republic, freedom requires exposure to a diverse set of topics and opinions. This is not a suggestion that people should be forced to read and view materials that they abhor. But it is a claim that a democratic polity, acting through democratic organs, tries to promote freedom, not simply by respecting consumer sovereignty, but by creating a system of communication that promotes exposure to a wide range of issues and views. *What if it doesn't and if it perils the regulatory powers you would give it?*

Libertarian

Nothing that I have said should be taken as an empirical argument about the likely choices of individuals in the next decades and more. Most of us have a great deal of curiosity, and sometimes we like to see materials that challenge us and that do not merely reinforce our existing tastes and judgments. This is demonstrated every day, not least by the truly astonishing growth of sites on the Internet. No one can know what many or most people will be choosing in the long-term or even short-term future. What I have attempted to do is not to suggest grounds for nostalgia or general pessimism, and much less to predict the future (in this context, an especially hopeless endeavor), but to explore the relationship between new technologies and the central commitments of a system of democratic self-government. Rather than being diverted by pessimism, nostalgia, and prediction, we should move beyond all three, in order to obtain a clearer understanding of our ideals, and to see what might be done to realize them.

FRANKLIN'S CHALLENGE

Recall Benjamin Franklin's answer to the large crowd asking the Constitution's authors what they had "given" to the

Think of Bush's paid reporters. Want to let that administration run a public information site?

that assumes he's right.
You've given no
indication that he is.

American public: "A republic, if you can keep it." Franklin's answer was an expression of hope, but it was also a challenge, a reminder of a continuing obligation, even a dare. His suggestion was that any document committed to republican self-government depends for its effectiveness not on the decisions of the founders, and much less on worship of texts and authorities and ancestors, but instead on the actions and commitments of its citizenry over time. In drawing attention to the dangers posed by an "inert people," Justice Brandeis was merely carrying forward Franklin's theme.

My most general topic here has been the preconditions for maintaining a republic. We have seen that the essential factor is a well-functioning system of free expression—the "only effective guardian," in James Madison's words, "of every other right." To be sure, such a system depends on restraints on official censorship of controversial ideas and opinions. But it depends on far more than that. It also depends on some kind of public domain, in which a wide range of speakers have access to a diverse public—and also to particular institutions, and practices, against which they seek to launch objections. Above all, a republic, or at least a heterogeneous one, depends on arenas in which citizens with varying experiences and prospects, and different views about what is good and right, are able to meet with one another, and to consult.

Emerging technologies are hardly an enemy here. They hold out far more promise than risk. Indeed they hold out great promise from the republican point of view, especially insofar as they make it so much easier for ordinary people to learn about countless topics, and to seek out endlessly diverse opinions. But to the extent that new technologies increase

poor idea

people's ability to wall themselves off from topics and opinions that they would prefer to avoid, they also create serious dangers. And if we believe that a system of free expression calls for unrestricted choices by individual consumers, we will not even understand the dangers as such. Whether such dangers will materialize will ultimately depend on the aspirations, for freedom and democracy alike, by whose light we evaluate our practices. What I have sought to establish here is that in a free republic, citizens aspire to a system that provides a wide range of experiences—with people, topics, and ideas—that they would not have specifically selected in advance.

unrestricted by a potentially manipulative, deceptive gov't driven by special interests inimical to the polity's best interests.

bibliographical
note

There is of course an extensive literature on the relationship between democracy and new information technologies. Within that literature, several works have especially influenced my presentation. This brief note is not intended to offer a comprehensive bibliography for the topics discussed in this book, but instead to describe some of the discussions that I have found most helpful, and also to provide an entry into the literature as a whole.

Andrew Shapiro, *The Control Revolution* (1998), is an excellent discussion of the implications of the general increase in individual control over communications. Shapiro's discussion covers a number of the questions dealt with here, but it ranges over a much wider territory than does this book, and it contains illuminating treatments of many questions that I have not discussed. I have also learned much from Lawrence Lessig, *Code and Other Laws of Cyberspace* (1999). Lessig's very different emphasis is on the dangers to freedom posed by private and public control over the "code," or architecture, of cyberspace. But Lessig also writes from the standpoint of deliberative democracy, and he provides a brief but highly instructive treatment of the potential problems of individual filtering. An excellent, somewhat technical discussion of fragmentation, and the circumstances in which it might occur, is Marshall Van Alstyne and Erik Brynjolfsson, *Electronic Communities: Global Village or Cyberbalkans*, available at *http:// web.mit.edu/marshall/www/Abstracts.html*.

Of the countless treatments of how to make the Internet a better ally of democracy, I single out Andrew Chin, *Making the World Wide Web Safe for Democracy*, 19 Hastings Comm. & Ent. L.J 309 (1997), and Noah D. Zatz, *Sidewalks in Cyberspace: Making Space for Public Forums in the Electronic Environment*, 12 Harv. J Law and Tech. 149 (1998). Chin offers an early empirical study of links among sites with different viewpoints. I have built on his method for my own study in chapter 3. Zatz provides an excellent discussion of the public forum doctrine and its potential role in cyberspace. A number of helpful papers can be found in *A Communications Cornucopia:*

Markle Foundations Essays on Information Policy (Roger G. Noll and Monroe E. Price eds. 1998). Peter Huber, *Law and Disorder In Cyberspace: Abolish the FCC and Let Common Law Rule the Telecosm* (1997), is a lucid, passionate argument for a position very much at odds with that defended here; I have learned a lot from Huber's arguments. Richard Morris's *Vote.com* also discusses the relationship between new technologies and democracy, but in a way that neglects the republican aspirations of the constitutional design. Tim Berners-Lee, *Weaving the Web: The Original Design and Ultimate Destiny of the World Wide Web By Its Inventor* (1999), provides an easy entry into some technical issues and also much illuminating background and many interesting observations. A lively, brisk overview of current issues can be found in Alfred C. Sikes, *Fast Forward: America's Leading Experts Reveal How The Internet Is Changing Your Life* (2000). A decisive response to the widespread view that cyberspace is not regulable can be found in Jack L. Goldsmith, *Against Cyberanarchy*, 65 U. Chi. L. Rev. 1199 (1998). An especially good treatment of the development of the Internet is John Naughton, *A Brief History of the Future: The Origins of the Internet* (1999).

On group polarization, emphasized in chapter 3, an excellent general treatment is Roger Brown, *Social Psychology* 200–5 (1986). A more recent overview can be found in Cass R. Sunstein, *Deliberative Trouble? Why Groups Go To Extremes*, 110 Yale LJ 71 (2000), and a predecessor paper, *The Law of Group Polarization* (2000), available at *http://papers.SSRN.com/paper.taf?ABSTRACT_ID=199668*. Valuable treatments of social cascades include Timur Kuran, *Private Truths, Public Lies* (1997); Sushil Bikhchandani et al., *Learning from the Behavior of Others*, J. Econ. Persp., Summer 1998, at 151; Abhijit Banerjee, *A Simple Model of Herd Behavior*, 107 Q. J. Econ. 797 (1992). On freedom of speech, the classic statement of the basic view defended here is Alexander Meiklejohn, *Free Speech and its Relation to Self-Government* (1948). Other, very different views are developed in many places, including Frederick Schauer, *Free Speech: A Philosophical Inquiry* (1991); Robert Post, *Constitutional Domains* (1995); and C. Edwin Baker, *Human Liberty and Freedom of Speech* (1993). C. Edwin Baker, *Advertising and a Democratic Press* (1993), is an especially valuable treatment of the extent to which consumers of information are often commodities, sold to advertisers, rather than purchasers.

notes

1. Alfred C. Sikes, *Fast Forward* 204, 211 (2000).

2. Id. at 25.

3. Numbers go quickly out of date, but as of 2000, nearly thirty million people have personalized a Web page, over ten times the number from 1998. Of those who use the Internet, fully 71 percent personalize a Website to receive more relevant content, often involving local topics; 65 percent personalize a site so as to allow it to "remember" their "preferences and interests, based on their inputs." See Kevin Mably, *Private vs. Personalization* 5 (2000), available at *http://www.cyberdialogue.com*.

4. See Nicholas Negroponte, *Being Digital* 153 (1995). See also Robert Putnam, *Bowling Alone* 177–79 (2000) for a brief but helpful discussion of "cyberbalkanization," which draws in turn on an illuminating paper by Marshall Van Alstyne and Erik Brynjolfsson, *Electronic Communities: Global Village or Cyberbalkans*, available at *http://wed.mit.edu/marshall/www/Abstracts.html*.

5. See, e.g., Martha Nussbaum, *For Love of Country* (1998).

6. The point is emphasized in Andrew Shapiro, *The Control Revolution* (1999), from which I have learned a great deal, and many of whose concerns, including fragmentation and self-insulation, are the same as those stressed here.

7. See Putnam, *Bowling Alone* at 218.

8. The best treatment of this point is Amartya Sen, *Development As Freedom* (1999).

9. For a valuable general discussion, see C. Edwin Baker, *Advertising and A Democratic Press* (1997).

10. See Lawrence Lessig, *Code and Other Laws of Cyberspace* (2000).

CHAPTER 2
AN ANALOGY AND AN IDEAL

1. Alfred C. Sikes, *Fast Forward* 210 (quoting Ken Auletta).

2. In some ways these developments are entirely continuous with other important social changes. The automobile, for example, has been criticized for "its extreme unsociability," especially compared with the railway, "which tended to gather together . . . all activity that was in any way related to movements of freight or passengers into or out of the city." George Kennan, *Around the Cragged Hill* 161, 160 (1993). Far more important in this regard has been what may well be the dominant technology of the twentieth century: television. In the words of political scientist Robert Putnam, the "single most important consequence of the television revolution has been to bring us home." Putnam, *Bowling Alone* 221. And the result of the shift in the direction of home has been a dramatic reduction—perhaps as much as 40 percent—in activity spent on "collective activities, like attending public meetings or taking a leadership role in local organizations." Id. at 229.

3. See Air Technology Groups Powers living.com, available at *http://industry.java.sun.com/javanews/stories/story2/0,1072,17512,00.html*.

4. Sikes, *Fast Forward* 208 (quoting Alvin Toffler).

5. *Hague v. CIO*, 307 US 496 (1939). For present purposes, it is not necessary to discuss the public forum doctrine in detail. Interested readers might consult Geoffrey Stone et al., *The First Amendment* 286–330 (1999).

6. See *International Society for Krishna Consciousness v. Lee*, 505 US 672 (1992).

7. See *Denver Area Educational Telecommunications Consortium, Inc. v. FCC*, 518 US 727, 802–3 (1996) (Kennedy, J., dissenting).

8. See the excellent discussion in Noah D. Zatz, *Sidewalks in Cyberspace: Making Space for Public Forums in the Electronic Environment*, 12 Harv. J Law and Tech. 149 (1998).

9. See *Columbia Broadcasting System v. Democratic National Committee*, 412 US 94 (1973).

10. An especially illuminating elaboration of republican ideals is Philip Pettit, *Republicanism: A Theory of Freedom and Government* (1999).

11. See Gordon Wood, *The Radicalism of the American Revolution* (1993).

12. From the standpoint of American history, the best discussion of deliberative democracy is William Bessette, The *Mild Voice of Reason* (1984).

There are many treatments of deliberative democracy as a political ideal. For varying perspectives, see Amy Gutmann and Dennis Thompson, *Democracy and Disagreement* (1998); Jurgen Habermas, *Between Facts and Norms* (1997); and *Deliberative Democracy* (Jon Elster ed. 1998).

13. A popular treatment is Dick Morris, *Vote.com* (2000).

14. To be sure, one of the central trends of the last century has been a decrease in the deliberative features of the constitutional design, in favor of an increase in popular control. As central examples, consider direct primary elections, initiatives and referenda, interest group strategies designed to mobilize constituents, and public opinion polling. To a greater or lesser extent, each of these has diminished the deliberative functions of representatives, and increased accountability to public opinion at particular moments in time. Of course any evaluation of these changes would require a detailed discussion. But from the standpoint of the original constitutional settlement, as well as from the standpoint of democratic principles, reforms that make democracy less deliberative are at best a mixed blessing. Government by initiatives and referenda are especially troubling insofar as they threaten to create ill-considered law, produced by sound-bites rather than reflective judgments by representatives, citizens, or anyone at all. For valuable discussion, see James Fishkin, *The Voice of the People* (1995).

15. 2 *The Complete Antifederalist* 369 (H. Storing ed. 1980).

16. *The Federalist* No. 81.

17. 1 *Annals of Cong.* 733–45 (Joseph Gale ed. 1789).

18. *The Mind of the Founder* 156–60 (M. Meyers ed. 1981).

19. Bill Gates, *The Road Ahead* 167–68 (1995).

20. *Abrams v. United States*, 250 US 616, 635 (Holmes, J., dissenting).

21. *Whitney v. California*, 274 US 357, 372 (1927) (Brandeis, J., concurring).

22. For more detailed discussion, see Cass R. Sunstein and Edna Ullmann-Margalit, *Solidarity in Consumption*, available at *http://papers.SSRN.com/paper.taf?ABSTRACT_ID=224618*.

CHAPTER 3
FRAGMENTATION AND CYBERCASCADES

1. Putnam, *Bowling Alone* 178.

2. See Sikes, *Fast Forward* 13–14.

3. Van Alstyne and Brynjolfsson, *Electronic Communities* 5.

4. Andrew Chin, *Making the World-Wide Web Safe For Democracy*, 19 Hastings Comm/Ent L.J. 309 (1997).

5. Id. at 328.

6. For a fascinating discussion, see Ronald Jacobs, *Race, Media, and the Crisis of Civil Society* (2000).

7. See Matthew Zook, *The Unorganized Militia Network: Conspiracies, Computers, and Community* 1 (1996), available at *http://socrates.berkeley.edu/~zoon/pubs/Militia_paper.html*.

8. Id. at 2.

9. See Roger Brown, *Social Psychology* 222 (1996). These include the United States, Canada, India, Bangladesh, New Zealand, Germany, India, Bangladesh, and France. See, e.g., Johannes Zuber et al., *Choice Shift and Group Polarization*, 62 J Personality and Social Psych. 50 (1992) (Germany); Dominic Abrams et al., *Knowing What To Think By Knowing Who You Are*, 29 British J Soc. Psych. 97, 112 (1990) (New Zealand).

10. See D.G. Myers, *Discussion-Induced Attitude Polarization*, 28 Human Relations 699 (1975).

11. Brown, *Social Psychology* 224.

12. D.G. Myers and G.D. Bishop, *The Enhancement of Dominant Attitudes in Group Discuission*, 20 J Personality and Soc. Psych. 286 (1976).

13. See id.

14. See Elisabeth Noell-Neumann, *Spiral of Silence* (1984); see also Timur Kuran, *Private Truths, Public Lies* (1997).

15. See Russell Spears, Martin Lee, and Stephen Lee, *De-Individuation and Group Polarization in Computer-Mediated Communication*, 29 British J Soc Psych 121 (1990); Abrams et al., *Knowing What To Think* 112; Patricia Wallace, *The Psychology of the Internet* at 73–76 (1999).

16. See John Turner et al., *Rediscovering the Social Group* 142 (1987).

17. Spears et al., *De-Individuation*.

18. See Wallace, *Psychology of the Internet*.

19. See R. Hightower and L. Sayeed, *The Impact of Human-Mediated Communication: Systems in Biased Group Discussion*, 11 Computers in Human Behavior 33 (1995).

20. Wallace, *Psychology of the Internet* 82.

21. Thomas W. Hazlett and David W. Sosa, *Was the Fairness Doctrine*

a "Chilling Effect"? Evidence from the Postderegulation Radio Market, 26 J. Legal Stud. 279 (1997) (offering an affirmative answer to the question in the title).

22. See Caryn Christenson and Ann Abbott, *Team Medical Decision Making*, in *Decision Making in Health Care* 267, 273–76 (Gretchen Chapman and Frank Sonnenberg eds. 2000).

23. Id. at 274.

24. See, e.g., Sushil Bikhchandani et al., *Learning from the Behavior of Others*, J. Econ. Persp. 151 (Summer 1998); Andrew Daughety and Jennifer Reinganum, *Stampede to Judgment*, 1 Am. L. & Ec. Rev. 158 (1999).

25. See Timur Kuran and Cass R. Sunstein, *Availability Cascades and Risk Regulation*, 51 Stan. L. Rev. 683 (1998).

26. George Johnson, *Pierre, Is That A Masonic Flag On The Moon?* New York Times, Nov. 24, 1996, section 2, p. 4.

27. See Mark Granovetter, *Threshold Models of Collective Behavior*, 83 Am. J. Sociology 1420 (1978); for a vivid popular treatment, see Malcolm Gladwell, *The Tipping Point* (2000).

28. See Lisa Anderson and Charles Holt, *Information Cascades in the Laboratory*, 87 Am Econ Rev 847 (1997).

29. Several of these examples are discussed in id. and in Granovetter, *Threshold Models* 1422–24.

30. See James Fishkin, *The Voice of the People* (1995).

31. Id. at 206–7.

32. Id.

33. James Fishkin and Robert Luskin, *Bringing Deliberation to the Democratic Dialogue*, in *The Poll with a Human Face* 23 (Maxwell McCombs and Amy Reynolds eds. 1999).

34. See id. at 22–23 (showing a jump, on a scale of 1 to 4, from 3.51 to 3.58 in intensity of commitment to reducing the deficit; a jump, on a scale of 1 to 3, from 2.71 to 2.85 in intensity of support for greater spending on education; showing a jump, on a scale of 1 to 3, from 1.95 to 2.16, in commitment to aiding American business interests abroad).

35. Id. at 23. See also id. at 22 (showing an increase, on a scale of 1 to 3, from 1.40 to 1.59 in commitment to spending on foreign aid; also showing a decrease, on a scale of 1 to 3, from 2.38 to 2.27 in commitment to spending on social security).

36. See, e.g., Bruce Murray, *Promoting Deliberative Public Discourse on the Web*, in *A Communications Cornucopia: Markle Foundations Essays on Information Policy* 243 (Roger Noll and Monroe Price eds. 1998).

37. Sikes, *Fast Forward* 15 (remarks of Paul Matteucci).

CHAPTER 4
SOCIAL GLUE AND SPREADING INFORMATION

1. See Sen, *Poverty and Famines*.

2. See Sen, *Development As Freedom*.

3. Elihu Katz, *And Deliver Us From Segmentation*, in *A Communications Cornucopia* 99, 105 (Roger Noll and Monroe Price eds. 1998).

4. For more details, see Sunstein and Ullmann-Margalit, *Solidarity*, on which I draw for the next paragraph.

5. See Putnam, *Bowling Alone* 18–24.

CHAPTER 5
CITIZENS

1. Robert H. Frank and Philip J. Cook, *The Winner-Take-All Society* 201 (1995).

2. Alexis de Tocqueville, *Democracy in America* 317 (1987).

3. John Dewey, *The Future of Liberalism*, in *Dewey and His Critics* 695, 697 (Sidney Morgenbesser ed. 1977).

4. See Frank and Cook, *Winner-Take-All Society* 19.

5. See Albert Hirschmann, *The Passions and the Interests* (1967).

6. See Jon Elster, *Sour Grapes* (1983).

7. See Robert Frank, *Luxury Fever* (1998) for a good discussion.

8. See id.

9. See id.

CHAPTER 6
WHAT'S REGULATION? A PLEA

1. John Perry Barlow, Declaration of Independence of Cyberspace, Feb. 9, 1996, available at *http://www.erf.org/pub/publications/John_Perry-Barlow/barlow_0296.declaration*.

2. If broadcast licenses were not allocated by the FCC, and if they

were a more ordinary form of property right, exactly the same would be true! Property rights as we know them are created and protected by government. Of course this is not an argument against property rights.

3. See Hayek, *The Road to Serfdom* 38–39.

CHAPTER 7
FREEDOM OF SPEECH

1. For more detailed treatments, see Cass R. Sunstein, *Democracy and the Problem of Free Speech* (1993); Alexander Meiklejohn, *Free Speech and its Relation to Self-Government* (1948); and C. Edwin Baker, *Human Liberty and Freedom of Speech* (1995).

2. *Virginia State Bd. Of Pharmacy v. Virginia Citizens Consumer Council*, 425 US 748 (1976).

3. 44 *Liquormart, Inc. v. Rhode Island*, 517 US 484 (1996).

4. See *Buckley v. Valeo*, 424 US 1 (1979).

5. See, e.g., Thomas Krattenmaker and L.A. Powe, *Converging First Amendment Principles for Converging Communications Media*, 104 Yale LJ 1719, 1725 (1995).

6. The old case, allowing government action, is *Red Lion Broadcasting v. FCC*, 395 US 367 (1969).

7. See, e.g., *Denver Area Educational Telecommunications Consortium, Inc. v. FCC*, 518 US 727 (1996). The Court's caution is defended in Cass R. Sunstein, *One Case At A Time* (1999).

8. See *Lochner v. New York*, 198 US 45 (1905).

9. For an effort in this direction, see Sunstein, *Democracy*.

10. See id. at 77–81, for an overview.

11. James Madison, *Report on the Virginia Resolution, Jan. 1800*, in 6 *Writings of James Madison* 385–401 (Calliallard Hunt ed. 1906).

12. I draw here on Sunstein, *Democracy* 132–36.

13. *Pruneyard Shopping Center v. Robins*, 447 US 74 (1980).

14. I attempt to answer it in Sunstein, *Democracy* 121–65.

15. The best discussion is Geoffrey Stone, *Content Regulation and the First Amendment*, 25 Wm. & Mary L. Rev. 189 (1983).

16. The murkiness of current law is illustrated by the Court's division in *National Endowment for the Arts v. Finley*, 118 S. Ct. 2168 (1998), where the Court upheld a statute directing the NEA, when making funding decision, to consider "general standards of decency and respect for the

diverse beliefs and values of the American public." The Court suggested that it would have ruled differently if the statute had discriminated on the basis of viewpoint.

CHAPTER 8
POLICIES AND PROPOSALS

1. A good discussion can be found in James Hamilton, *Channeling Violence* (1998).

2. See Neil Gunningham et al., *Smart Regulation: Designing Environmental Policy* (1999).

3. See Frank and Cook, *Winner-Take-All Society* 203 (1995).

4. See Shapiro, *Control Revolution*.

5. *Red Lion Broadcasting Co. v. FCC*, 395 US 367 (1969).

6. *Miami Herald Publishing Co. v. Tornillo*, 418 US 241 (1974).

7. *Turner Broadcasting Co. v. FCC*, 520 US 180, 227 (1997).

8. Id.

9. Id.

10. See Chin, *Making the World Wide Web Safe*. For criticism and related proposals, see Zatz, *Sidewalks*. There is a widespread view that regulation of the Internet is not possible; a decisive response can be found in Jack L. Goldsmith, *Against Cyberanarchy*, 65 U. Chi. L. Rev. 1199 (1998).

11. See id.

CHAPTER 9
CONCLUSION: REPUBLIC.COM

1. John Stuart Mill, 3 *Principles of Political Economy* 594 (1848).

2. John Dewey, *The Public and its Problems* 168 (1927).

acknowledgments

This book grows out of two lectures: the inaugural lecture for the Center on Law and Public Affairs at Princeton University and the closing keynote address for the symposium at Kent State University on the occasion of the thirtieth anniversary of the May 4, 1970 killings on that campus. I am most grateful to my exceptionally generous hosts on those occasions. At Princeton, particular thanks go to Stephen Macedo, Amy Gutmann, and Robert Willig for their hospitality, their comments, and their questions. At Kent State, I am especially thankful to Thomas Hensley for his kindness and for helpful discussions. Faculty and students were extremely helpful on both occasions.

I am grateful above all to my editor, Thomas LeBien, for helping to give the book its basic direction, for general encouragement, and for superb suggestions. C. Edwin Baker, Mary Anne Case, David Estlund, Jack Goldsmith, Stephen Holmes, Martha Nussbaum, Eric Posner, Richard Posner, and David Strauss provided valuable suggestions and advice. Considerable help also came from four anonymous reviewers for Princeton University Press. Brooke May and Lesley Wexler gave superb and creative research assistance. Chapter 3 draws on my essay, *Deliberative Trouble? Why Groups Go To Extremes*, 110 Yale LJ (2000), and I thank the *Yale Law Journal* for editorial help and for permission to reprint some sections of that essay here.

index

ABC television station, 129, 131, 149

"access rights" (must carry) rules, 182–84, 185

Advanced Research Project Agency (ARPA), 132–33

African-Americans: communication enclaves used by, 193; cybercascade on spread of AIDS among, 81; print media aimed at, 61; Web sites specifically designed for, 57–58

AIDS cybercascades, 81, 82–83

Alien and Sedition Acts, 155

Amazon.com, 23, 135, 168, 185

American Civil Liberties Union ratings system, 55

American Conservative Union, 16

American Prospect, 11, 136

American Visions magazine, 58

argument pool: depolarization and shifts in, 79–80; enclave deliberation growth of, 76; limited discussion group, 68

ARPA (Advanced Research Project Agency), 132–33

Auletta, Ken, 23

Barlow, John Perry, 128

Basketball Weekly, 11

Bell, George, 7

Bill of Rights: first Congress rejection of original, 41; Jefferson vs. Madison over value of, 42–43. *See also* U.S. Constitution

Bloomingdales.com, 24

Bohnett, David, 54

Boston Tea Party discussion group (hypothetical), 51–52

Brandeis, Louis, 46, 98, 155, 174, 183, 201

Breyer, Stephen, 183

Broadcast.com, 5–6

"Bullet 'N' Board" (NRA discussion group), 52–53

Buy.com, 24

CBS television station, 129, 130, 131, 137, 149

censorship, 8, 195, 201

CERN, 133

Chinese famine (1950s), 89–90

Cigar Aficionado, 11

citizens: benefits of shared experiences to, 95–96, 193; consumer's interests vs., 114, 122; consumer sovereignty and relationship of consumers to, 49–50, 106–7, 195–98; heterogeneity vs. homogeneity of, 9, 40–42; limiting

citizens (*cont.*)
opportunities of, 110–13;
link between well-being/free
expression by, 90–91; republican government designed to
serve, 195–96; unanimity and
majority rule of, 116–17
Citizens Against Government
Waste, 16
Clinton, Bill, 82
Code of Conduct, 177, 178–80
collaborative filtering, 25–26, 168
commercial speech, 143–45
communications system: consumer
sovereignty as goal for, 106–
7; declining role of intermediaries in, 11–13; with/without
enclave deliberation of, 75–
79, 192–95; fairness doctrine
of, 73–75, 175, 182, 183; increasing regulation of, 128–
31; Mill and Dewey on value
of, 191–92; requirements for
free expression in, 8–10; social role of, 89–91; solidarity
goods through, 94–96; spiral
of silence pattern and exposure to, 68–69; suggestions
for future trends in, 198–200;
technology and personalization of, 5–10; threat of digital
division of, 20–22; unacknowledged public forums by
intermediaries of, 34–37. *See
also* regulation
computer viruses, 125–26, 141
Conservative Coalition ratings system, 54–55

Conservative Political Action Conference, 16
consumers: citizen's interests vs.,
114, 122; freedom and relationship of citizens to, 49–50,
106–7, 195–98; as Internet
commodity, 18–19; Internet
growth and demands of, 117–
22; preferences/beliefs of,
107–10, 112–17
consumer sovereignty: compared to
political sovereignty, 44, 45–
46; consumers and citizen relationship and, 49–50, 106–
7, 195–98; democratic institutions and exercise of, 113–
15; First Amendment protection of, 143–45, 146–51;
preferences formation/defor-
mation and, 107–10
consumption treadmill, 117–22,
195
Contract law, 137–38
Cook, Phillip, 109, 178
copyright law, 145
cybercascades phenomenon: described, 49, 80–81; impact
of Internet on, 81–84; "tipping point" phenomenon and,
83
cyberspace "sidewalks" proposal,
189
"cyberterrorism," 134, 197

"the Daily Me," 7, 12, 22, 44, 50,
192, 194
Declaration of the Independence of
Cyberspace (1996), 128

deliberative democracy: filtering and, 26, 198–200; First Amendment and, 153–59; and republicanism of U.S. Constitution, 37–39, 105, 200–201, 209n.14

deliberativedemocracy.com (deliberativedeocracy.org) [hypothetical], 170–71

deliberative domains, 170–72

deliberative opinion poll, 84–87

democracy: citizen well-being/free expression link in, 90–91; dangers of fragmentation to heterogeneous, 87–88; filtering in a, 10–13; free expression requirements and, 8–10; impact of personalized communication on, 7–10; overview of filtering issues and, 13–16; preferences and, 122–23; promoted through voluntary self-regulation, 178–79; public forum doctrine of, 27–37; republic compared to, 37–39, 197; severing link between free speech and, 146–47. See also deliberative democracy

depolarization, 79–80

Dewey, John, 44, 109, 110, 190, 191–92

digital divide: as international threat, 20–22; Web sites which increase the, 57–62. See also group polarization phenomenon

disclosure requirements, 172–77

discussion groups: fragmented free speech by, 51–53; group identity and, 69–71; group polarization phenomenon and, 65–69; hate, 53; limited argument pool of, 68; social comparison mechanism and, 68–69; specialization of, 54–56. See also Internet; Websites

Dog Fancy, 11

Dole, Robert, 129

Domain Name System (DNS), 133

Duke, David, 82

Econline.com, 58

Electoral College system, 39

Elster, Jon, 111

e-mail: development of, 132–33; viruses spread through, 125–26, 141

enclave deliberation: group polarization and, 75–77; public sphere and, 77–79

EPCRA (Emergency Planning and Community Right-to-Know Act), 172

ESPN.com, 58

Excite search engine, 7

fairness doctrine, 73–75, 175, 182, 183

famine, 89–90, 91, 102–3

FBI (Federal Bureau of Investigation), 130, 134

FCC (Federal Communications Commission), 74, 173, 183

"57 Channels (and Nothin' On)" (Springsteen song), 56

filtering: collaborative, 25–26, 168; by Constitutional government structure, 38–39; defining issues of, 17–22; in a democratic society, 10–13; implications of growing power of, 8–10; overview of political/freedom issues and, 13–16; suggestions for limiting ability to, 198–99; technology impact on consumer, 3–5; three difficulties with, 48–50. *See also* fragmented communications

Finley, National Endowment for the Arts, 211n.16

First Amendment: conclusions regarding, 165–66; consumer sovereignty and, 143–45, 146–51; democratic deliberation and, 153–59; examining flaws in current view of, 151–53; "must carry" rules promotion of, 183. *See also* U.S. Constitution

Fishkin, James, 84, 86, 170

Fourteenth Amendment, 150

fox and the sour grapes fable, 110–11

fragmented communication: basis of concerns about, 57; as danger to heterogeneous democracy, 87–88, 192; described, 48–49; fewer shared experiences due to, 97–98, 193; impact of links/hyperlinks on, 184–86; Internet and free speech, 51–54; limiting filtering ability to limit, 198–200; three fundamental concerns regarding, 167–69. *See also* filtering; policy reforms

Franklin, Benjamin, 105, 200–1

Frank, Robert, 109, 120, 121, 178

free choice: as communications evaluation criteria, 195; consumer sovereignty and, 113–15; formation/deformation of preferences and, 107–10; regulation vs., 127–28; relationship of consumers and citizens and, 49–50, 106–7, 195–98

free expression: Holmes vs. Brandeis opinions on, 46–48; impact on preferences by, 110; Internet and fragmentation of, 51–54; link between well-being/social goals and, 90–91, 198; The Nuremberg Files Web site and, 141–42; overview of filtering and issues of, 13–16; as part of self-government, 155–59; public forum doctrine and, 27–37; regulation of, 138–40, 141–43, 144–45, 160–63; two requirements of, 8–10; undermined by limited information, 110–13

free speech: commitment to deliberative democracy and, 153–59; as not being "an absolute," 151–53, 198; principles of, 145–51, 153–54, 166; severing link between democracy and, 146–47; three forms of neutral regulation over, 160–63

free speech laws: applied to The Nuremberg Files Web site, 141–43; governing commercial speech, 143–45; on limits of political dissent, 46–48; protecting the public forum, 27–28; subsidies and penalties of, 163–65

Gates, Bill, 44, 86, 143, 146–47
general interest intermediaries: described, 34–37; in a free society, 196–97; information dissemination by, 101. *See also* media
geocities.com, 54
Goodman, Jack, 148
goods: information as public, 99–102; solidarity, 49, 94–96
government: consumer sovereignty and democratic, 113–15; examining regulation motivation of, 157–58; Fourteenth Amendment limiting regulation by, 150; free communication as central part of self-, 155–57; freedom of expression limitations by, 141–42; opportunity/information restrictions by, 110–13; penalties and subsidies by, 163–65; regulation through property rights laws of, 129–31; unanimity and majority rule in, 116–17. *See also* policy re-

forms; regulation; republican government
group polarization phenomenon: depolarization and, 79–80, 192; described, 65–69; fairness doctrine and, 73–75, 175, 182, 183; group identity reinforced by, 69–71; the Internet and, 71–73; pros and cons of, 75–77. *See also* digital divide

"hackers," 134
Hamilton, Alexander, 40
hate discussion groups, 53
hate group Websites, 62–64t, 65
heterogeneity society: building solidarity in, 93–96; citizen homogeneity and, 9, 40–42, development of just, 109–10; fragmented communications and dangers for, 87–88, impact of shared experiences in, 91–98, 193; information as public good for, 99–102, 103; maintaining a republic, 200–2; thought experiment to explore, 78–79
HIV cybercascades, 82–83
Holmes, Oliver Wendell, 16
homogeneity society, 9, 40–42
hyperlinks: attention and, 184–86; possibilities of policy reform using, 187–89

information: cybercascades phenomenon and, 49, 80–84; deliberative opinion poll

information (*cont.*)
and, 84–87; difficulties with
filtering, 48–50; freedom undermined by limited, 110–13;
Internet spread of, 90–91; as
public good, 99–102, 199;
shared experiences and, 91–
93, 98–99, 193; social glue
through spread, 103. *See also*
filtering
information overload, 56–62
Info Xtra, 6
institutions: consumer sovereignty
and democratic, 113–15, 197;
preferences/beliefs as product
of, 109–10; property rights to
protect, 138–40
Internet: consumers as commodity
of, 18–19; consumption
treadmill and growth of, 117–
22; creating deliberative domains on the, 170–72; deliberative opinion poll on the,
85, 86; fragmentation of free
speech on, 51–53; free choice
vs. regulation of, 127–28;
groupism and information
overload by, 56–62; group
polarization on the, 71–73;
growth/percentage of .coms,
118t; history of regulation of,
134–38; history of the, 132–
34; implications of "must
carry" rules for, 184, 185;
links to allies/adversaries on
the, 59t; mixed blessings of
the, 23–25; "personalized
shopping" on the, 25–26;
property rights laws applied
to, 134–38, 156–57, 197;
public forum doctrine prac-
ticed on the, 28–30; "sidewalks" proposal for, 189;
spiral of silence pattern and
exposure to, 68–69; spread of
information through, 90–91.
See also discussion groups; technology; Websites
Intertainer, Inc., 7

Jefferson, Thomas, 43
just society, 109–10

Katz, Elihu, 92
Kennedy, Anthony, 29

Lessig, Lawrence, 19–20, 136,
137
LEXIS, 187
limited argument pool, 68
links: attention and, 184–86; possible policy reforms using,
186–87
Love Bug computer virus, 125–26,
141
lungcancer.com, 24

Madison, James, 43, 155, 201
magazines. *See* print media
majority rule, 116–17
Mbeki, President, 82–83
media: Code of Conduct for, 177,
178–80; disclosure requirements for, 172–77; fairness
doctrine applied to, 73–75,
175, 182, 183; as intermediar-

ies of unacknowledged public forums, 34–37; "must carry" rules and, 182–84, 185; ratings system for, 173, 176–77; regulation through property rights of, 128–31; solidarity goods through, 94–96; spiral of silence pattern and exposure to, 68–69; "tabloidization" trend of, 177–78; traditional freedom of choice in, 60–61

Melanet, 58

Mill, John Stuart, 191

minority rights, 116–17

Moonves, Leslie, 147

Movielens, 25

"must carry" rules, 182–84, 185

MySimon.com, 24

NAB (National Association of Broadcasters), 148, 149, 175

National Endowment for the Arts v. Finley, 211n.16

national holidays, 93–94

National Review, 11, 16, 188

National Rifle Association's "Bullet 'N' Board" discussion group, 52–53

National Science Foundation, 133

NBC television station, 129, 149

NEA (National Endowment for the Arts), 164, 211n.16

Negroponte, Nicholas, 7

Netzero.com, 19

newspapers. *See* print media

Newsweek, 12

New York University, 24

Noell-Neumann, Elisabeth, 68

North, Oliver, 16

NRA (National Rifle Association), 149

"The Nuremberg Files" Website, 141–42

Oklahoma City bombing, 52, 53

Oliver North Radio Show, 16

"open code" movement, 20

Pathfinder.com, 58

Patriot movement, 63

PBS (Public Broadcasting System), 180–81, 182

penalties, 163–65

personalized communication market, 5–10

"personalized shopping," 25–26

PICS (WWW Consortium's platform for Internet content selection), 54

Playboy.com, 58

policy reforms: deliberative domains as, 170–72; disclosure as, 172–77; using links/hyperlinks for, 184–89; "must carry" rules as, 182–84; six possibilities listed for, 169–70; subsidies as, 180–82; tyranny of the status quo and, 190; voluntary self-regulation as, 177–80. *See also* regulation

political sovereignty, 44–48

Practical Horseman, 11

preferences/beliefs: consumer sovereignty and exercise of, 113–15; democracy and, 122–23; formation and deformation of, 107–10; majority rule interference with, 116–17; as product of options and choices, 112–13. *See also* consumers

President's Advisory Committee on the Public Interest Obligations of Digital Television Broadcasters, 147, 148–59

priceline.com, 117

print media: aimed at African-Americans, 61; falling circulation rates of, 13; regulation through property rights of, 130–31; traditional freedom of choice in, 60–61; as unacknowledged public forum intermediary, 34–35

productopia.com, 24

property rights laws: applied to Internet regulation, 134–38, 156–57, 197; as necessary to free expression, 138–40, 144–45; regulation through, 129–31

Protect Americans Now, 16

Public Broadcasting System, 164

public forum doctrine: changing nature of modern, 196; described, 26–27; enclave deliberation and, 77–79, 192–95; on exposures to experience vs. arguments, 33; limiting boundaries of, 28–30; "must carry" rules and, 182–84; three goals of, 30–34; unacknowledged intermediaries of, 34–37; on unplanned vs. unwanted exposure, 32–33

public interest groups, 176

Public.Net (proposed), 181

Qrate.com, 25

radio media, 174, 176, 177, 182

ratings system, 173, 176–77

Raymond, Eric S., 136–37

regulation: examining motivation of, 157–58; Fourteenth Amendment limitations on, 150; free choice and, 127–28; history of Internet, 134–38; as necessary to free expression, 138–40, 141–43; promoting public interest goals for TV, 147–50, 154; subsidies and penalties of free speech, 163–65; television and legitimate, 145–46; three forms of neutral free speech, 160–63; through property rights laws, 129–31, 134–38, 156–57, 197; voluntary self-, 177–80. *See also* government; policy reforms

republican government: benefits of heterogeneity to, 40–42; conditions for maintaining, 201–2; as Constitutional intent, 37–39, 105, 200–1, 207n.14; democracy compared to, 37–39, 197; designed to serve citizens, 195–96. *See also* government

Second Amendment, 149
Sedition Acts, 155
Sen, Amartya, 89, 198
Shapiro, Andrew, 181
shared experiences: consumers/
    producers of information and,
    98–99; fragmentation and
    fewer, 97–98; national holi-
    days as, 93–94; societal bene-
    fits of, 91–93, 95–96; soli-
    darity through social glue of,
    93–96, 103, 193
Sherman, Roger, 41, 42
"sidewalks" proposal, 189
slavery institution, 109
social capital, 97
social comparison mechanism, 68–
    69
social problems: famine as, 89–90,
    91, 102–3; information as
    public good and, 99–102;
    role of communication in,
    89–91; shared experiences
    and, 91–93, 193
society. *See* heterogeneity society;
    homogeneity society
solidarity goods, 49, 94–96
Song Online, 58
Sonicnet.com, 6
sovereignty concepts, 44–48, 49–
    50
"spiral of silence," 68
Springsteen, Bruce, 56, 57
status quo tyranny, 190

subsidies: compared to penalties,
    163–65; as policy reform,
    180–82

"tabloidization" trend, 177–78
Talkleft.com, 60
technology: the great promise of,
    201–2; impact on consumer
    filtering by, 3–5; link between
    social changes and, 208n.2;
    public forum boundaries and,
    29–30; sovereignty through,
    135–36. *See also* Internet;
    Websites
Telecommunications Act (1996),
    173
television: consumer vs. citizen's in-
    terest in, 114; disclosure re-
    quirements for, 172–77; im-
    pact of government control
    over, 92–93; legitimate regula-
    tion of, 145–46; "must carry"
    rules and, 182–84, 185; prop-
    erty rights as regulation of,
    129–30; regulation to pro-
    mote public interest goals,
    147–50, 154; regulation vs.
    free choice argument over,
    127–28; as unacknowledged
    public forum intermediary,
    35–36
Terrorist's Handbook (Internet
    posting), 52
Thomas, Clarence, 144
Time magazine, 12, 131, 189
"tipping point" phenomenon, 83
Titanicmovie.com, 58
TiVo, 6, 57

Tocqueville, Alexis de, 109, 110
Tony Brown Online, 58
Toxic Release Inventory, 175
tyranny of the status quo, 190

Unorganized Militia, 63
U.S. Constitution: Fourteenth Amendment of, 150; free speech tradition of, 155–57; heterogeneity and design of, 40–42; Jefferson vs. Madison over, 42–43; republicanism/deliberate democracy of, 37–39, 105, 200–1; Second Amendment of, 149; trend to decrease deliberative features of, 207n.14. *See also* Bill of Rights; First Amendment

v-chip, 173
Virtual Colleges, 24
viruses (Love Bug), 125–26, 141
voluntary self-regulation, 177–80

Wall Street Journal, 5
Warmaster's posting, 52–53
Washington Post, 131

Websites: consumer demand and growth of, 117–22; cyber-cascades spread by, 81–83; growth/percentage of .coms, 118t; historical development of, 133–34; links/hyperlinks of, 184–89; number of personalized, 205n.3; property rights and regulation of, 134–38, 156–57; proposed Public.Net, 181; publishing names of abortion doctors, 141–42; run by hate groups, 62–64t, 65; which increase the digital divide, 57–62. *See also* discussion groups; Internet
Weekly Standard, 11
Wexler, Lesley, 59
White Pride World Wide Website links, 65
White Racial Loyalists, 63–64
Wood, Gordon, 38
World Wide Web, 133. *See also* Websites

Zatso.com, 6
Zatz, Noah, 189